DANIEL B. MARTIN

Archway Publishing books may be ordered
through booksellers or by contacting:

Archway Publishing
1663 Liberty Drive
Bloomington, IN 47403
www.archwaypublishing.com
1 (888) 242-5904

Because of the dynamic nature of the Internet, any web addresses or
links contained in this book may have changed since publication and
may no longer be valid. The views expressed in this work are solely those
of the author and do not necessarily reflect the views of the publisher,
and the publisher hereby disclaims any responsibility for them.

Any people depicted in stock imagery provided by Thinkstock are
models, and such images are being used for illustrative purposes only.
Certain stock imagery © Thinkstock.

ISBN: 978-1-4808-2595-6 (sc)
ISBN: 978-1-4808-2596-3 (e)

Library of Congress Control Number: 2016900184

Print information available on the last page.

Archway Publishing rev. date: 2/12/2016

PREFACE

Having studied Philosophy in an academic setting, through books of my own choosing, by way of lectures available online, and throughout my life during every single experience I have ever had I think that most importantly one's own conception of Philosophy is unique and entirely relative to the development of their personhood. Philosophy is the way in which one understands life and the reality one perceives. I question what separates philosophy and life, and what separates philosophy from non-fictional literature. I will be introducing here my 'American Perspective of Existentialism', phenomenology, and pragmatism. These themes of focus are culminated through a travel diary I composed over the course of travels, short essays, and abstracts. It is intended to be experimental in nature.

Recorded here are my thoughts on existence and my human experience, keep in mind that they are just ideas and thoughts; read them or don't read them, consider them or don't consider them, find them valid or reject their validity- regardless they are my thoughts and expressions of my conscious stream through different points during my undergraduate studies in philosophy. They are meant to shed a light on my perspective, and as ideas for consideration. Please note with attention that nothing in this book should be taken as static and/or concrete. Enjoy...

INTRODUCTION

What a vast array of emotions we as human beings feel and such an incredible multitude of experiences which we incur through our existences! Each individual is a unique entity of being or unit-hood. Each of whom has their own unique set of experiences, a unique perception of events, a unique expression of self, and a unique outward effect upon all of existence. As a human being I take humanity very seriously. Thusly the subject of the human conscious experience is that which I find to be most philosophically fascinating and perplexing.

I like to try to project myself into the world I interact in, in many different ways. I remember once thinking, day dreaming really that if we humans are what we appear to be, a highly capable intellectual species, then we should exercise our intellectual capacities. We should embrace the possibilities and in doing so expand our minds. Our minds have been expanding since our birth observing and encoding into memories all that we have cumulatively experienced. Arguably the first step in anyone's conscious self-evolution is education. Education is not merely something which is administered to a conscious subject, it is the knowledge which the conscious subject apprehends and takes for their self. The 'knowledge' provided by a traditional education is but such relatively small thought fragments of the actual world, constituted as absolute truths by authorities of education. Your knowledge is most frequently gauged in school by how well you can regurgitate the facts that have been spoon fed to you. The process on paper seems simple; in a traditional education these fragments of truth are force fed into students, and the students are expected to memorize, repeat, and comply.

In the more romantic view of knowledge one's knowledge should instead be personalized and the information made relative to their own experiences'. These fragments are collected over time as one is educated both by life and by traditional schooling and the conglomeration of the fragments forms one's cognitive conception of reality. The most basic learning in a humans' development is the sensory experience and empirical data gathering which begin before formal schooling. Which I believe is why we refer to early childhood as one's *formative years*.

We first begin to recognize our capacities by way of our memory. Prior to development of linguistic thinking we are able to recognize the faces of our families. Throughout a lifetime of subjective consciousness the memories form into a tangled web of coding for stimuli and normative reactions to stimuli created by past experiences. Memory and our consciousness there-of offers us the ability once linguistic reasoning is begun to abstract and to reflect upon our experiences in an intelligent and cognitive respect. That is that in order to reflect upon something we must firstly observe it. When we reflect upon that sensory observation and apply linguistic symbols upon it we effectively renegotiate our memory of it so that it may be contemplated and also expressed to another subjective consciousness. The expression of one's own conscious existence to another self-aware being whom has their own conscious subjectivity is called communication. When we review experiences through contemplation we have the opportunity to change our perspective and our feelings about our experience.

I recall one day when I was sitting in the Japanese Zen Garden on the campus of UH Manoa. I could hear the Manoa stream rushing just on the other side of the trees, the whole hillside so vibrant, green, and teeming with life. I sat there observing the koi fish, when the notion came to me that, 'Just as koi fish swim about a pond and suck up algae so too should we humans wander where we can and absorb the world around us'. Some of our most inspiring talents as humans lay in our complexity of comprehension, our propensity towards symbolic reasoning, and the resulting capacity these talents provide for communication and cooperation.

Every day new experiences fall into our tangled cognitive web, and contemplation is the active cognitive process in which both the sub-conscious and the conscious work together to attempt to make some sort of sense of it all, establish what normality is, and as an accidental side effect create our conceptions of truth and knowledge. Since we determine these ideals within ourselves, after our experience and through our internal reflection, aspects of what we derive to be 'truth' can be shared- but ultimately these are individually and personally relativized ideas based off of concepts we form of our own experiences.

Since all humans seem to formulate these self-created notions of a 'true' normality, we are each bound to our own experiences. Yet, there is so much of existence that is not bound to us; namely all of those things which we have not yet experienced. The aspects which lie outside of one's conceived normality are not only limited to the external level of observed stimuli, but as well we will experience weird internal stimuli. Weird internal stimuli such as the emotions connected to things which do not fit neatly into our previously construed perspectives of normality- things which cause us to feel unprepared and to feel existential malaise. Or the feelings of maturation or physical illness which were not available to the consciousness in the past, but are developing into the spectrum of one's conscious awareness.

The more consciously active we are the more information we are gathering, and the more information we are attempting to process and relativize. I may be wrong but I sometimes wonder if some humans spend much of their existence turned off, or rather never turned on. In being as such they avoid developing a vibral and intellectual sensitivity of that which surrounds them; their consciousness having never expanded to fortify a direct route from the world into their minds. A pathway of reality from that which actually exists, twisted into their individually relative perceptions of the reality of actuality.

It is difficult to undergo a Husserlian épochè, an attempt to welcome newness, and to analyze under unbiased eyes. To allow openness towards that which has not by the individual been previously experienced- To expand consciousness into a greater relative understanding of the subjective consciousness and its connection to the universe through the conscious experience of life. I will start from the beginning of a time when I was so flooded by newness of experience that I could not help but start to write down the results an épochè which was enforced by environmental change, like that which happens when traveling to places you have never been before.

THE BEGINNING

December 11

My flight home was by all means a wondrous adventure in itself. Just prior to take off from a hill from whence smoke often rises, overlooking the twinkling lights of the Orange city, a guide of a nature foreign to most sailed through the overlying clouds of grey, and stringing henceforth from her flap did I see a thread of crystal. A crystal ball indeed did fall upon my head, awakening me once more from far too deep a slumber. So I rose up to follow my guide.

The weights slowly lifted from my collar as I chased her through the moonlit abode. We flew by through the star filled sky, and my mind began to wander. I glanced below at the old rough road, my guide allowed me to slow, and thankfully for a moment to stop. For by flew

1

another who would not. Quickening to old pace we flew round the bend, she turned... eyes beaming, my soul receiving, the beginning, not end.

The Only Constant

Life much like all else in the universe is subject to changes. Life shifts, and the things that are now are not the way which they used to be in the past, and are not the way which they will be in the future. We humans have the ability to reflect, and in doing so, we can connect the times of the past as they funnel into our future actions through the moment of now. As these changes in actuality occur, the human mind apparently must adjust itself in the re-appropriation of certain past ideals, perhaps even discarding some of those which are no longer useful.

The Jungle, in Kalapana on Hawai'i Island

December 21

All through the day and night the heavens unleashed their watery fury upon the land. Those same heavens which at night bless so kindly the land with their light, now drench the land in wet kisses. The cock moved by the occasion let out a loud cock-o-doodle-do towards the falling skies. What a storm, what an adventure. The trees howling; their cries echoing out of the forest below. The ground loudly applauds its' blessing with a clap, the pitter-patter-pitter-patter of drops forming fresh dew. I would have come here long ago. If only I had known.

Sometimes the elemental forces of a storm can be so strong that flooding occurs and the land itself can even begin to slide. After the storm the land is altered and never able to return to the same precise position as before the storm. Humans can as well experience emotional landslides, instances in which something so major happens that we can never return to the positions and ideals that we held before its occurrence. Depending on the situation and the person this can be either a horrible curse, or a fantastic blessing. Regardless of the things lost by change, some things seem to always return to the human being- most hopefully their sense of humor.

I presume it to be natural and even healthy for one's consciousness of these types of fluctuations to become apparent in one's life. Engaging with certain people or in certain activities can help to provide a balance, enthusiasm, or motivation for life. One should then, make efforts to indulge oneself in these persons or activities which make one happy. When actively analyzing your environment you will in time start to realize where the imbalances are coming from. You will sense the sources which cause you to feel so uncomfortably weird to yourself at certain points in your life. I believe that you will often find a causal factor be it an object, person, or habit which is causing this imbalance and the resulting emotional instability. You may have to put these things which are causing your instability aside for some time, while you work on other areas of your existence. This is a natural process of attachment and detachment. I wonder if the soul which is truly liberated can weather these types of transitions between attachment and detachment as they arise.

I wonder as well if the responsibilities that we obtain

throughout our lives are naturally occurring, or if they are entirely derived from choices that we humans made at some point during human evolution, and if there is a difference between the two. I wonder if our entire basis for ethics and morality is something actually shared from common origin or if they are coincidental similarities which arose independently in different cultural evolutions. The 'society' I was raised in in Southern California would suggest that people have to gain more and more responsibilities at different ages when they are mature enough to handle them. This same perspective of responsibility accruement exists in every society I can think of across the world. Does this commonality arise from a certain point in our ancestral past? Or is it logic which brings us to the realization that each individual should accumulate more and more responsibilities until a certain point when they are too old and the responsibilities begin to taper off. How forceful cultural evolution is when expectations from one society are applied to all of its diverse individuals.

Perhaps the process of cultural/social-evolution is more fluid and adaptive to the changes in the universe if the individuals continuously revise them- In revising one takes control, they become a subject in the world and not solely the object of a subjective society. If they are contagious revisions then by accident the individuals donate their own ideas to society. This method of consciousness focusing on the self and letting the energy of the self-flow outward from the self would flow more smoothly if we were not bombarded by society's authoritarian assertion of fear. There exists today such a prevalence of propaganda being constantly barraged against the subjective individual consciousness. The attack is all too effective at diminishing the individual human's possibility for liberation and imaginative creativity by forcing conformity with the previously contrived notions of other individuals from different places and past times.

I wonder what powers as imaginative and potentially productive beings do we have; I am questioning to what extent are we actually empowered by our own consciousness? If we are empowered, then what can we do if we do not also have the liberty to use our empowerment? And if we did have the liberty to use it, what kinds of consequential responsibilities would arise in connection and relation to the liberties? Lastly and also are some individuals naturally more liberated or empowered, or is liberation and empowerment entirely a conscious decision which the individuals make for themselves? I will leave those questions open and unanswered.

July 24

Just as the individual gains responsibilities as they grow older, so does the human race incur ever more responsibility as it ages. We age with the earth like two close friends, interdependent our whole existences, neither wanting to see the other die first.

There is no stress in life except for that which one creates in their own mind. So for one to find answers one must disallow themselves from the illusion of stress.

A great goal of man is to reconnect with nature, and thusly to reconnect with themselves. Man came from nature, so man should serve nature, and in return nature shall serve him.

I think that quite possibly the most liberating and most damning of human sentiments is love. Love is one of the greatest sources of energy that humans have to pull from. We use our love of many things to motivate us towards certain items, people, places, or actions. I would sincerely hope that all humans are fortunate enough to experience as many forms of love in their life as is possible. Love adds color and beauty and even masks some of the uglier things, the things that we don't like to accept exist, yet which exist independent of acceptance. Those negative things which we may choose to paint over with something more positive, something optimistic and something imaginative yet very real to the individual. We can cover things with love for the good of the thing being covered, and for our own good as well.

Nick, my roommate in college began an experiment which I joined in on. The idea of the experiment was to re-place the world 'fuck' with love. Anytime we felt compelled to rhetorically utilize the word fuck for any purpose what-soever, we would replace it with love. For example, "Love! This chapter is so hard to read!" or perhaps, "This tastes so loving good!" It seemed silly at first but we realized that the energy we were putting our intentions towards was not trapped in our thought spaces. It was in fact spilling out into our environment. It was hard at first but after a while it became a habit. I would like to think it is a habit which I can pick back up. Such strong forces can be exerted by society, something as amazing as replacing a negative word with a positive word is ridiculed out of practice because it is different. Such fear creates no room for liberation to thrive.

December 25

In review of the primary steps of cognition we find again that the first step is observation, the empirical gathering of information and the encoding of this information into the individuals memory banks. The second step is reflection, the investigation and relativization of experience and knowledge. Again we must remember that our talents lay in our complexity of comprehension, our symbolic reasoning, and the resulting capacities for communication and cooperation. Thirdly we can think and act intelligently off of the knowledge we gain from our experience and the ideologic forms of knowledge gained from the reflection and internalization of that knowledge. In doing so if we manage to act rightfully we will retain our dignity and we make evolutionary progress whether it be for the evolution of the self or for society.

We work freely within our own perspective; our choices are governed by our options. We want to choose what we can when we can. We may at times amidst a vast field of options and choices feel compelled to reflect asking, 'Where are we going?' These answers change day by day. The screaming idealist in me wants to advise myself and everyone else to live, day by day... Wake up to new dawns, new horizons, new possibilities and explore them- for by the morrow they will be but a memory of yesterday. That idealist in me can be so loud an idealist, but I cannot ignore him for he has too valid a point.

Time is not limited, and in time all things change. What are limited are our subjectively conscious existences, our lives, and our opportunities. The hard part of humanity is the suffering we experience when we feel the effects of circumstances in which we feel we have little to no power. We often feel lost, hopeless, and scared. Do not fear.

Thrust into life at birth we are forced into the reality of change. I believe it would be wise and beneficial to stay positive in all situations. Life is not always easy, but we can make it pleasureful, we can find happiness even after long periods of seemingly inescapable darkness. That is if we really will to be happy more-so than we are afraid of being unhappy.

Rejection of the reality we are subjected to can cause pain. Allowing acceptance of change is a solution to easing the suffering. It is our ignorance, desires, and emotions which blind us from the true reality (actuality)- the chains which bind and limit us from reaching our full potentials. If only we can be strong and wise enough to see through our distractions, into a more pure state of being. Then we would know what is. And so I ask you because I do not know yet surely for myself: What is?

The Downside

December 26

The reflection process, learning, and growth can all be very existentially painful. Our ideas and beliefs construct our realities. When our realities are shattered it can be very arduous to pick up the pieces and make any sense out of them. If the journey were easy however, it would not be as rewarding. The concept is as ancient as it is harsh; our pains strengthen us as we overcome them. We still crave control, and we crave understanding. But I think that most of all we crave love, happiness, and liberation.

What can we do? Survive. We have to make it through these hard segments and persevere. We have to look out for our immediate needs, and find the surplus from deep within our souls to weather the storms in life. Honesty and sincerity are two beautiful virtues. Sometimes we find it hard to be honest with ourselves during the reflective process. We want to find the painless way out of our misery, perhaps there is no painless way out, and pain and suffering are unfortunate by-products of our human evolution.

January 2

Times turn and seasons change, the reality of a new year and a new adventure rests at my feet. I can fight or be fought, beat or be beaten. Instead I close my eyes and wander… into the inevitable future.

The creatures of the night begin to crawl shortly after the sun sets. Even in darkness the earth is alive, moving and breathing in the cold night air. Peace can be hard to find by day, but in the deep silence of the night, while women and men sleep, it lingers out there roaming in the empty woods and streets. It hides in the darkness out of sight and out of our minds.

Do we ever have anything in life? These things come and go as if we never really had them. Our dreams which once floated so far away, seemingly unreachable, come to us and just as quickly fade away. Does life not do the very same? Comes to us like a dream and fades away off into the passing of time.

January 10

I would like to take a moment to share some of the things which my friends were talking about at the time I was writing in this notebook. I think it is important to express a glimpse into the curious environment I was in at this crucial stage in my own self development.

"There is a difference between men whom wear hats because they are bald, and those whom are bald but wear hats." – Max Dosland

"What if everything were just compactals of fractals, exploding and shimmering before our very eyes" – Jordon Bennett

And one quote from myself. 'Freedom, what is freedom anyway? Does anybody know? If I were free, what else would I be? What would I feel and see? If I were free…'

Life without forgiveness is like eating the air off of an empty plate for supper. It lacks substance, depth, and causes me to question your cooking. Forgiveness is an important aspect of love. Without it love is a jagged sword, which bleeds all of those around it.

January 14

It is amazing the changes in one's life, how they can in retrospect be classified into periods. In certain periods we had certain mindsets, emotions, goals, dreams. While aspects can be shared by and through periods, there is something which we noticed changed over certain stretches of time, namely our perspective of our experience changed. A 'period' may last a moment, a few days, or years, but at some point it fades into another period, one in which we may not agree with an older constituted version of the self. We may want something so badly during one period, and then in another period reject that very same thing.

What bridges lay between what we want and what we get? I think it might be our determination or our focus. The degree to which we want what it is that we think we want, and how much we are willing to sacrifice to get it are what lay between our imagination and getting what we want. There have been, are, and likely always will be some physical limitations as to what a person can imagine. Yet, over time with proper attention we as cognitively active humans may manifest our desires (metaphysical alchemy). There exists a potential possibility for positivity (or unfortunately negativity) effecting the universe, of effecing our own existences', and the existences' of others and other things which is so incredibly immense. Our potential impact through cognition upon the world literally vibrates out into the environment around us. This outward impact or 'outpact' is very similar to the mystic idea of ones aura, a certain wavelength or pattern of energy emittance that a particular person or object emits.

Could it be that if we stay determined, if we can keep sight of ourselves in all different situations and in many different lights, then we can carry on; we can continue to keep making those changes which we view will make the world more beautiful according to our own ideas and preferences?

On the Art of the Slow Walk

Slow walking is an idea introduced to me by my friend, and later roommate Max Dosland. Max is from Maui, and there is hardly ever a reason to be in a rush on Maui. Myself being from California walked a great deal quicker than Max. One night as we were leaving the gym, he pointed this out to me and said, "What you Californian people don't understand is that I can walk as quicky as you if I wanted to, but I don't want to. And I bet it's easier for me to walk fast than it would be for you to walk slow." Challenge accepted! I moved as slow as I could, stepping from side to side. Max was amused, and in encouragement he said to me, "When you are in a rush, you are only focused on where you are going, and you turn all attention away from where you are. The more slowly you move the more conscious and aware you become of all of those things around you." He was right, and for some time I would slow walk when possible, either on the way home from the gym, or back to my apartment after class. Some people looked at me like I was ridiculous, I didn't care, I was doing my thing. After some time of conducting these experiments I conjured up the following reflection;

The importance of where it is that I am going fades as I experiment with slow walking. The emphasis of attention turns to where I am, what is around me and sown deep a connection between the two. We are not, or should not be in a rush. What a shame it would be to rush through and past one's own life. When traveling slowly, the mind slows as well and clarity is more simply obtainable. Where are you?

January 24

The very essence of our being is strong and powerful. Through life we disconnect from ourselves, we lock on and attempt to process all of the splendor and the pains which surround us. We lose sight of ourselves, even becoming afraid of the powerful self within. Contemplative self-reflection is an important step in the knowing of one's self. To know oneself is to love oneself. When living a life centered on self-love, how could one help but find love everywhere, to open up to the beauty of life, no longer feeling the need to hide. I ponder what it is about ourselves which scares us so. What it is that makes it so hard to begin the journey, and for the quest of life to truly be fruitful. Perhaps self-doubt once seeded in the mind is a ferocious weed to battle.

Passion if it is possessed in life does not evaporate, but frequently life requests us to heave piles of dry dirt atop it, giving it a dull and saturated appearance, yet at the core of it lives, and it holds through time waiting to be unearthed.

January 26

Legs tremble onward, pushing through the pains, I have searched and found and left it all, now carrying only myself. What a heavy burden to bear. My mind focuses on being exactly what I am, an adventurer treading on a foreign land, deeply connected, out of the thick and into the sand…

In reflection it is wise to be honest, even at the times when it hurts. The truth is out there and it wants to be found- even if we can never find it, we should still search.

I fear the prospect of not living more so than I could ever have to fear from life itself. Although some facets many be dark and unpleasant at times, at least during life they are observable and we are able to experience them. This is the gift of cognitive human life. On va vivre pour la belle vie.

To get lost is to allow yourself to have the potential of being found, or to find your own way. Try to get lost, ask questions that have no apparent answers, and never be too certain amidst the winds of change.

February 4

Often times the yearning for control and the sense of having control influences my thoughts. The practice of self-discipline is seemingly universally helpful in the pursuit of happiness which we humans embark upon. It is far too common that humans are raised without developing a mature sense of self-discipline. When the mind has been tempered it responds more smoothly, and ideally as well the body can act with a higher degree of efficiency and effectiveness as well since it is controlled by the mind. Discipline like all things is relative to the individual and their circumstances, but certainly some cultivation of self-discipline is undertaken by all persons. I guess the question is of the quality and degree of the cultivation.

February 26

If the law of physics which states that for all action there is a corresponding reaction is true, would you not want to be the cause of good actions? What a grand experience life is. Nothing is still, nothing is at rest. When you move you groove! Good actions start with good thoughts. So Stop! Think 'good' and resume your orbit

These are the things we all must tell ourselves at times, to motivate us towards the things which we aspire. It may seem cheesy but do we all not have moments of our lives where we look in the mirror and tell ourselves something inspirational? In doing so we are offering ourselves something to get the energy going, and to attract the things we want in life. Do we not occasionally as well turn a blind eye to the opportunities that present themselves?- caving in and surrendering as an object, to a great fear of the unknown, left immobilized, pathetic, and weaker than we are. These are the moments in which we would greatly benefit from being conscious and reminding ourselves of all that we are capable of; Happiness. This may require some creativity, a little dramatic exaggeration, whatever it is that it takes to motivate.

March 10

Healing is a process, it has many stages. Some of these stages hurt and others feel good. If you can manage to keep sight of your direction, you can heal all wounds- in time.

People are beautiful and friendship a gracious act. What a beautiful grace life takes on through friendship. Keep getting yourself lost, and keep finding new friends.

Intensity, the vibrancy of life, the power of chance. What awe of life I am struck with today. With smoke on the mountain and water running in the stream. I dream the day dreamers dream. Never sure of what is actually as real as things may seem.

Time

Although humans operate with their daily lives revolving almost entirely around clocks, I posit that most would be hard pressed to offer an accurate definition for time. Time seems at first sight to be a physical principle- a very basic physical principle at that. All changes we discuss occur over observed periods of time. But is primal time in the sense of a progression of changes, external to observation, not adhering to a perceptual and perpetual passage of moments really the same time exhibited on a clock? This concept of primal time attempts to access the essence of time, preceding the definition. This primal time would be the changes which occurred in a valley which has no consciously subjective occupants. Precipitation would at times fall, and at other times not fall. The plants and trees of this valley would go through periods of gestation, growth, flowering, death and decay regardless of there being a subjective unit to observe the changes which occur over the flow of primal time. Regardless of measuring the roughly 24 hours that it takes the earth to complete its rotation, there is a series of changes which occur in primal time, that we only later with instruments of measurement compute into the concept of time in a 24 hour day, broken up by hours, minutes, seconds, milliseconds, etc.

Certainly movement exists. What began movement and its primal functionalities are incomprehensible by our human spectrum of cognition. The 'beginning of time' was so incredibly long before life began, before the earth existed and certainly far before creatures inhabited the earth, and even longer still than when the human intellect began to evolve. Yet it is the first moment where movement occurred, that movement setting forth all of the chains of causality between the moment now and the 'beginning of time'. Before the movement everything currently in existence very well may have existed in some physical sense, yet until movement began, the possibility for 'time' had not. Time for humans is different than primal time. We model our concepts of time off of our perception of primal time. We say that a second is such and such a length, a min, hour, day, week, year, century, etc. Yet, this is just one calendar model out of many which have been created around different cultures perceptions of times. We even state these periods in English whereas there can be equally as culturally or individually relative expressions for these passages of primal time in any subjective consciousness. As for clocks, midnight is not usually the actual center of the period of darkness. Sunsets and sunrises, moonsets and moonrises occur at different times every day. This is true for all areas of the world. And so in our attempts to simplify the true randomness of change we use linguistically expressive symbolism.

Scratching our heads out of confusion over our formal systematization of time we have a lot to consider. Are we not still surprised to see the sun peak up over vast ocean, plain, or mountain each *time* we experience its *occurrence*? Do we not marvel at the moon *when* it is at its fullest and brightest? We could be locked in a dark room from which we do not escape and regard on an electronic tablet that it is 6:45 a.m. and that the sun is now rising on the exterior of this room, and sit there in some form of contentment which neglects the wonderment of actually experiencing the sunrise because we saw digitally the correlation of time as a measurement and a description of time as an event. Would we not in doing so rob our spirit of something that is uniquely acquired by our consciousness through real experience? We can make these secondary associations and descriptions without actually having witnessed the event of which the time placement associations are formed by looking at data, even data formulated by another person or computer system. However, we cannot through secondary accounts re-cognate the primal frequency resignations which existed only in the experience itself.

We humans seemingly place time structures around actual events and later in our recantations and remembrances of these events think that we can in some way use our secondary linguistic intelligence to convey to them as anything nearly as magnificent of an experience as that primal experience which we are attempting so fleetingly to convey.

Our intellect is so powerful that it can imagine bridges so long we could never cross them. We have such powers working for and against us. These separations of will are what lead us into existential struggle rather than into pragmatic existentialism. Pragmatic existentialism should be a celebration of the self- that utilizes the power of this intellect, and the liveliness of the body in carrying out the whims of the intellect for the greatest good. Our own minds are so powerful that within them we can either make or break any obstacle. Our own mind even chooses the mode of approach, and many of the factors associated with the creation and removal of these cognitive obstacles. Words- like gods and goddesses, have the power to reach out and move subjects, and thusly to move objects in the physical world. We can hear them and find their associations with other ideals like strength, courage, patience. But yet, even these types of powerful and virtuous words and understandings are just that; words, those same words which desperately try to grasp on to that which is prior to them, the primal experience.

So what is time? We may never really know. I think that regardless of any definition offered, each individual has their own conception of what time is even if it is arduous to put this conception into words. We will likely be told time and time again to refer to clocks and calendars in search for this answer. Despite all of this technical confusion, I am certain that so long as we humans are living we will experience time. And from our experiences we will form memories laden with linguistic representations of time so that we may at least share the portions of time experience which are communicable and valued. For such appears to me to be the nature of humanity in regards to time-cognition.

April 11

The road to nowhere has a certain freedom granted by its ambiguity. The ambiguity grants the road infinite possibilities, rather than defining it and expecting its own essence to hold up to the thoughts created in attempt to describe the experience of that essence it is free to be its own essence, unrestricted.

April 14

"Of what have we spoke, just next to now?"
"Is it fun to play with your identity?"
"What is self-development?"

When exploring consciousness I think it is good to get creative, ask questions that might seem odd. You may not in doing this always find the most pertinent answers to your most dire questions. What you may find instead, is a stretching of your minds ability to ask questions and to see the same thing from a number of perspectives without ever leaving your own subjective consciousness. This is called multi-dynamic perspectivism. The above examples are just a few of the more perplexing questions that my friends, colleagues and I came up with during conversations.

On Liberty

In order to 'be free', one must...? Is freedom really contingent? Or is freedom merely an idea? - An aspiration? Liberty as I am defining it is freedom as an escape from some confines. Balance then is the key to the universe! The key of balance here would be to have just enough liberty to actually be free, and just enough freedom for the freedom not to be contingent upon something else. All of our mistakes in life are rectifiable through time, a positive mindset, and with love. There is no need for worry, no need for doubt. Instead life asks of us gentle loving understanding.

What then are we to make of all these thoughts, all these internalizations of interactions with the external? This is for each individual to assess and determine for themselves. I think that I want a world which is beautiful to me, full of the people, places, and things which I enjoy most, and I want the liberty to lovingly engage with it. I may not really know what any of them are. In fact, I may be limited in perspective so much so that I do not even realize what or who I am. Despite these lack of cognitive access to the primal world I will always be processing, and always be learning about things, myself, and the relations between subjects and objects.

What Does it Matter?

April 20

Essence without form has no function,
Form without essence has no capacity,
Existence is not without unity.
We are all subjects of existence,
Thinking beings capable of a life of excellent happiness.

Dipped in sweet chocolate, sprinkled with nuts;
Life should be enjoyed, before it melts and fades away.
The currents all converge into one ocean,
An energized massive force which is the origin of the
possibility, as well as a host of life.

Acting as a powerful unifying force which recedes,
Only to crash again,
Pounding against its' own existence.
Forever changing yet its' being endures and it pours
itself upon the earth, over and over again.

I think we have a lot of power in terms of deciding what parts of things which actually occur are those which we choose to accept and supplement into our conceptions of reality. We certainly have many of choices in life. At least we do when we are in a state of liberation. Assuming that we are in a state of liberation we can select from multiple possibilities for all types of instances. This is an example of how an act of liberation comes with it a naturally instilled responsibility. If we from the field of possibility choose something, we cannot go back in time and un-chose it, once it is said it is said, and once it is done it is done. This can have horrifying or fantastic consequences, again depending on the individual and all the corresponding relative factors. Ideally if we educate ourselves, and constantly reflect these new ideas through the knowledge we already hold, constantly reassigning our conceptions of reality, we can shift through these stages in life, and make the best decisions relative to our subjectivity, our objectivity, our environmental conditions, and to other subjects as well.

On wants

April 28

What do we end up with if we deny ourselves all of the pleasures of life?
A form of dull existence.

What do we arrive at by selfishly pursuing only our pleasures?
A wasted existence, void of humanity.

A few questions I think that humans should always contemplate and endlessly readdress are; where do we draw the line? How should we act given all that we think that we know? What is moral action? What is the ethical answer?

If we spend all of our time wallowing, mopping around in our fortress chambers we allow ourselves to get lost in our own disillusions. We reject the beauty of life, turning our backs on possibility after opportunity time and time again as we shut doors and lock all the locks.

When in reality we should have very little to fear, and everything to hope for.

Many humans live a life of confusion, their actions revolving in a constant state of reaction. Unaware of our own subjectivity we are unable to shape the direction of our subjective existences. We decline our subjectivity and offer ourselves up only as objects.

To be lost; does this not happen to all humans at some point or another. We start to feel as if we are losing sight, or that what we have sight of might not be quite what we had assumed it to be. When we lose our sense of direction we can become disoriented. This can either be channeled into new experiential learning, or it can send one into a chasm of fear. We presumably choose which direction of the two we are going to go into, but when fear attacks those whom are lost, the choice is lost, and we begin to run where fear chases us. We then lose our liberation; and eventually in shedding our liberation we become the prisoners of fear.

People often have similar fears such as the fear of losing one's own life or the fear of self-death (Arguably the most natural fear), fear of losing loved ones, fear of being disowned by groups or individuals, fears of failure, fears of being wrong, fears of being inadequate, fears of all kinds of types and natures which seem to naturally occur in subjects. Moreover, what the individual choses to do in reaction to the fear is where I would expect the true character of the individual to be revealed.

The journey of a lifetime can give you a vast ever-changing perspective on humanity, the world, and how the two interact with each other. Even in familiar situations in which our brains are trained to respond we can feel uncomfortable and highly awkward. When traveling through different regions, states, countries, and continents you come face to face with things that you never expected to experience. This can make you feel completely human, or completely uncomfortable in your own skin. I like to take chances, and do things that are different if I think that there is a substantial amount for me to gain in life experience for undergoing such a feat. Moving to Hawaii for college was certainly one of the largest endeavors I chose to take on, and I did so wholeheartedly, that is not to say however that I was not fearful of my future, fearful of reality and at times very uncomfortable. In time, it became normal for me. It replaced my tendencies which I had acquired from Southern California.

It was the summer of 2013, after my finals and all course work was completed I temporarily moved out of my dormitory on campus, placing all my belongings in a storage locker I shared with fellow philosopher and dear friend Mathew Williams when I began another stage of my journey.

Part Two

GOING PLACES

With a lifetime of reading and thinking topped off by a few semesters of academic philosophy under my belt I could not help but dream. I would have these elaborate fantasies of knowledge and the liberation it could usher in. Of a future far different from anything like what we humans now experience. I would imagine a world not of routine and cyclical practical business, economics, exploitation, suppression, and suffering but rather dreaming of a world where love and the honesty are fundamental to a compassionate currency for an economics of humanity. The *intentionality* is important here- which kind of wealth should we be attempting to gain through our experiences? If thought actions and physical actions are constantly ruled by the will to be monetarily wealthy then both life and humanity at large will constantly be diminished and replaced by selfish intentionality making its casual passage into the environment of physical actuality.

Before I could be certain if these dreams were my own, or if they were a more frequent commonality of other persons, I needed to revisit the world.

Live whilst you are alive and be dead when you are dead. With so much left to see and so many things left to do... When you are dead, what will they say you did?

May 5

I handed over my key card to my dormitory resident advisor and a few hours later my brief experiment with vagrancy began. I wanted to distance myself from my familiar concept of having a home and a bed I call my own. Ideally by wandering the island of Oahu and not knowing where I was going to sleep, I would better handle the unfamiliar circumstances I may find myself in farther down the road during my summer's travels. First, I went to the local health food store, grabbed a plate of pasta salad with tofu and a coconut water. Yes, really roughing it...

I then took my food outside and sat down at a table and began to eat; unsure of what the future held and ready for adventure. King Street in Honolulu was busy as usual with trucks, cars, mopeds, bikes and pedestrians streaming by. Before I finished my meal an old Kanaka (Native Hawaiian) man, possibly permanently homeless himself, but possibly as well just pushing a shopping cart down the street stopped, looked at me and said, "Aloha" with great zeal and exuberance. I returned the exact same sentiment towards him. He continued on to tell me that not only was it, "A beautiful day" but also that, "today is a day blessed by God." I smiled and agreed that it was beautiful and that the sun was extra intense; because of the solar intensity of this early summer day everything seemed unusually vibrant.

He smiled back and gave his Aloha again, and then he walked up to the next table where two middle aged women were sitting, chatting and eating. Being in this instance just as polite and friendly as when he approached me did he give his aloha and smile at them. Lost in their disconnectedness from their fellow humans, they ignored him. His response to this disrespect was, "Fucking ha'ole!!" and he walked off continuing as he had since the moment I had first caught sight of him.

I think that in order to build a friendly community, full of understanding and compassion you have to emotionally get over some of your preconceived notions about life, your conceptions of normality, and expectations of the actions of other people. There are so many things which to your own conscious realm of experiential reference seem 'normal'- meanwhile those same things seem bizarre to other persons and other cultures conceptions of normality. Why not expand your frame of reference? And perhaps become slightly more connected to existence in the process.

When you travel to other cultures lands, you find yourself at odds wresting with your comfort zones and challenges of your conception of normality. As a potential consequence of millennia of human social evolution the very state of our spirits' (if there is such a thing, and we have them) are hindered when we are unable to openly and honestly share ourselves and to take in the energy of others around us in an exchange of consciousness. Perhaps a remedy may come about through experimenting with having an open heart to complete strangers.

Why strangers? They are persons with whom you have no previous expectations of, determinations for, or emotional connections towards. Furthermore, they occupy a physical space within a proximity of possible interaction such that one has the choice to be kind or unkind; in the pragmatic pursuit of goodness one should attempt actualize their best capacities whenever possible. Virtue capacities such as kindness extend outward and improve the condition of your immediate environment through positive intention in interaction. Ideally when you remove fears and doubts you find that there is no reason to not extend yourself through extending your energy.

May 14
When things die their spirit does not, or so I think.

Lightening stuck a large tree atop Pu'upia. The tree has slid down the hill some ways and has made itself an obstacle on the path up, as well as on the path down. As I approached the tree I could still feel its spirits energy. It vibrated and I swore I could sense it moving, morphing, its' surface fluctuating. Its' spirit does not want to leave its' place upon the hill here in the beautiful Manoa Valley on the island of Oahu. At the moment neither do I... In the back of this wide valley strong winds or 'Makani' blow constantly and rainfall is frequent. Countless trees line the slopes and ridges of the valley.

While I was enjoying the view from the grassy hill atop pu'u pia a few other travelers crossed my path. They approached in a fit of hearty laughter, enjoying life and a beautiful day together. It was a group of English speaking Japanese travelers and they asked me to take their picture. I obliged recognizing the potential for me to help others capture their moment of happiness. Kindness to strangers is so simple, whenever the negative prejudices of one party are removed enough to initiate a positive interaction, the positive interaction has the potential capacity to develop into something wonderful and good. Afterwards, they headed back down the path, and I headed back down into my reflection.

Last night I slept on a beach towel spread out on a park bench at Kapiolani Park on the side of Diamond Head, a looming dormant Volcano. I recall being quite aghast at the beautiful star filled sky above me. I found peace in the simplicity of the moment, a lack of need, detachment- perhaps.

I remember thinking of how I have been told many a time how lucky I have been all my life to have had safe places to sleep, a loving family, and my basic needs met. There are so many people without these necessities and even more without the luxuries that I have been blessed with in life. A major factor motivating this experiment with vagrancy was to tap out of what I had been conditioned to expect, to want, and what I was convinced that I needed. I wanted to know what it would be like to be disconnected from my expectations of material comfort, and to go walking through the big city looking for a place to sleep for the night.

During my brief experiment with vagrancy things were quite uneventful. I learned only one thing from that night of real importance, a person does not need a home but it's both comfortable and convenient to have one; especially if said home has a bathroom with a toilet, a shower and hot water. My experience was short lived, but it gave me a more refined appreciation for the things I always have had- both the necessities and the luxuries.

We begin in ignorance as to who we may run into on our adventures. Those persons we may meet at chance, whom we may teach, and who may teach us something as well. There is so much to see and to feel and so much to reflect upon. First I must meditate and ease my mind. Only two days left until I leave Hawaii for the summer, only two days left of being vagrant in Hawaii.

I posit that perhaps sometimes we must take a step back before we can leap forwards; such is the nature of change. I was heading out to Hawaiian sacred grounds Wai'Akea'Akua falls high in the mountains of Oahu. Rarely traveled to, it peacefully rests as one of the most beautiful clear falls on the south side of the island. The falls are themselves a sacred site on which Kane drew forth from a rock the spring from which flows the 'water of the place of the gods' whom are said to reside just above the falls atop Mount Olympus.

On my way up, I was tested. I hike barefoot because I enjoy the softness of the ground and the squishes of the mud between my toes. There are few dangers to walking barefoot through nature in Hawaii; in fact I find barefooted-ness aids in traction. I was meditating and singing trying to focus the intention of my journey the entire path up, step by step. There was a root on the ground, sticking straight up from the path. It was severed at a near 45 degree angle. I had not seen it before I placed my right foot upon it. My weight had already shifted into that foot before I realized that my foot was being impaled by the root. It shot up and struck one of the bones connected to my toe, it was incredibly painful, and unexpected. Luckily the root had gone straight in and out, leaving a thin but deep laceration. It was hardly bleeding, so I continued climbing, I was already nearing the falls, and didn't want to abandon my purpose.

Someone else was here not long ago. They brought their prayers up here to the gods. Tied rope from the Aina (land) to a rock and preformed their rites and rituals with the objects. Myself as well came here to call upon the Hawaiian gods; Kane, Kanaloa, Ku, and Pele. I gave to them three prayers.

As is customary I tied a ti leaf around stones from the stream. The first of which was porous and imperfect, yet round and strong. I saw it as a reflection of myself. I asked for guidance from Kane, a blessing for my journey, and to say Mahalo (thank you) for everything I have received on my journey thus far.

The second was for past love; Kailani. I found a small smooth rock, and collected a tea leaf to wrap around it. It had become clear to me by now that human confusion and selfishness had dispelled a once amorous connection, as it often does. I could not ignore my thoughts on this subject, even though they may seem somewhat illogical. These intuitive feelings which often come to me in dreams, told me that she is my souls mate through past life, after life, and in this life as well. I decided that there was the possibility, If not in this life in our next, I will have the opportunity to make up for the selfishness. I asked for forgiveness from the gods, from her, from myself as well, and also for their blessing upon her spirit.

The third is for my younger brother, and my family in California. I asked the spirits of the forest, 'Aumakua, to assist them, as I imagined I had been assisted in my life during tough times. Partway through my prayers I had noticed a beautiful colorful mountain bird had flown down. It perched on a rock a few feet in front me and witnessed my prayers. I decided I should take this as a sign that my prayers were at very least heard, and would be taken up to the gods by the bird. After taking a dip in the top most pool I departed back down the mountain.

Religion and spirituality, whether real or just projections of wishful human consciousness can be an immensely powerful force in persons lives. If we are honest towards a deity or deities, we are also then being honest with ourselves, and that in itself is powerful. This self-honesty may not always be easy to achieve without supplementation of the displacement that occurs in the act of imaging a relationship and interaction with external spiritual forces such as those often personified as deities. *My next logical step* is to choose to continue on in my life appreciating what I have when I have it, because these things we take for granted and may think are permanent are not; all things are all subject to change.

An Essay on Chronomatic Systematization

All of the things which we do are ruled by chrono-cyclical systems. Our circadian rhythm determines that we sleep for some time, at the end of that period we wake and then we are awake for some time. Again, at the end of this waking period we find ourselves falling back asleep. Thus completing one full chrono-cyclical cycle that is referred to in English as a day. Our needs fall into these cycles as there are times at which we are hungry, we then eat, and eventually are no longer hungry. This period as well is followed by a period in which we have not thoughts about food. All of this so that only later we can be once more hungry and undergo the relatively similar actions in order to move about through the segment of the cycle of which we are in. The same goes for attending school or work. We have systems and times at which we are at work and at play, and other times at which we are not in either. Thus the changes of consciousness during different segments in these cycles display our conscious humanity resting on the fringe of these changes. Changes which inevitably occur, yet our realities as constituted by time through chrono-cyclical systems retain some degree of repetition, regularity and predictability. Yes, quantum consciousness.

Perchance as a result of this perceived regularity even when we find ourselves amidst newness we are still trapped in the expectancies of previously experienced chrono-cyclical systems; such that we may operate for some time not adequately augmenting our realm of cognitive experience by openly incorporating the spirit of newness. But rather thinking and acting over reliantly upon our old platforms of reality and normality. All of our natural needs are addressed by primary chrono-cyclical systems; namely, our drives for food, water, shelter, and human interactions. We humans are fortunate in that we have cognitive access to the analysis of these cycles. Theoretically, if we contemplate and analyze these cycles we gain cognitive designership in our perspectives' of life, the world and our place within it.

Plants in their chono-cyclical patterns are synchronized with the rising, shinning, setting, and absence of the sun and its light. As well with the less regular but still cyclical changes in weather such as rain and wind. Their entire life and the possibility of what they may be are governed by the changes initiated by these cycles. Life in this cyclical understanding is much the same with animals as it is with plants. Upon the first breaking of day the birds awake and begin their daily searches for food, once they have gathered enough to ensure their survival and the procurement of their offspring they can attend to their social pursuits. These chrono-systems ultimately govern the survival of all life species. As well, humans must have the means to complete tasks necessary for survival and given that these tasks are performed with ease there is a surplus of time within a day's cycle in which pursuits of pleasure superfluous to survival may be undergone.

On Traveling

May 16

It may be fun to travel with a friend, but many times people must travel alone. In my perspective I am enjoying traveling solo because I feel more-free in my decisions and have the whole world to meet during my travels. I can stop and see anything I would like, and I can wander down any road without the requisite of group approval and planning. Despite the appreciation of my alone time I had a great deal of fun on Oahu cruising to the West Side with my friends Katie and Zach, North Shore with Kanoe, and East Side with Max Dosland. I am shifting and meditating on the changes that will arise as I begin this next leg of my journey which I must now take alone.

At Honolulu International Airport I met nice people in line. I find it hard not to try to connect with others around me when waiting for things in public, operating as a line friend to other humans I find myself temporarily situated near. I digress. Truth be told, I was finding it emotionally hard for me to leave Oahu, especially for such a long duration. This small island paradise has become my home, and my emotional connections to the land, atmosphere, and people run deep.

I find that I enjoy learning about the variety of life and life styles from those whom I meet while traveling and branching out. I met in line a woman whom lives in California. She was standing with her father who lives in Kohala on the Big Island of Hawaii. She informed me that she had studied in France when she was younger and thusly she shared in my excitement for my trip. We shared our pasts, futures, goals and pleasant memories during our random acquaintance. Of course I recognize that I could have just stood in line quietly feeling fearful and self-conscious, not connecting with anyone.

I managed for a moment to stand blissfully and patiently in line awaiting my turn to go through the security post. That is until I took conscious note of another couple waiting in line with their sister and her baby. They stood out to me because I had noticed an act of kindness they performed towards another traveler. They had allowed him to cut ahead of them in the security line because his flight was to leave in 30 minutes. I saw this random act of public kindness and decided to lend not a literal hand yet a metaphorical hand in the form of my loud voice to help him out and move farther up. I found myself kindly shouting to the whole of the line that this man is in a great hurry and could use their assistance in allowing him to pass them prematurely in line. They all let him pass. I was glad.

I made it to my seat at gate 25 of Honolulu International Airport seat 26G. In my experience in this seat I had found sitting next to me a couple from San Diego, they as well were very friendly. They had come to Hawaii for three days on a free time share vacation. They were also kind enough to share some red wine with me; it's beautiful when strangers extend their experience and their blessings to others to ease the harshness that we face in our conscious existential humanities. In fact most of those sitting near had entered into our conversation, eventually they passed their free wine glasses my way, totaling 6 plus my own, their kindness coupled with the wine made for a much more comfortable flight! Aboard the plane there were lots of kind vibes and my dreaded departure was playing out against my initial expectations. I should not be so quick to assume that I know what any experience will hold until it has passed and I have opportunity to reflect upon it in retrospect.

Of all of those whom I met while aboard my flight to Los Angeles I felt as though I had really connected with a man sitting across the aisle from me. The man sitting across from me was a classic example of a Hawaiian uncle from Kailua. What I mean by that is that he was well humored and full of Aloha. He was accompanied by his wife who is from Hilo on the Big Island of Hawaii. They were traveling with their son to Los Angeles to see him off to his first year of school at the University of Southern California. They were so proud of their children's accomplishments, as their other son is an engineer with a 'good job' in Honolulu. I was informed that this uncle owns a boat, and is a fisherman. He told me a few of his favorite fishing tales of the old days before overfishing began. I suppose one never knows what pleasant interactions may arise when love is the governing principle in a relationship- even if it be a love extended towards strangers; humans grow out of environments of love to do wonderful things with their humanity. Besides was not everyone a 'stranger' before you first met them?

I find myself reflecting on the community that occurred, as silly as it may seem to the reader, that all the persons sitting around me as they handed over their wine. I was so thankful for their communal support given the state I was in. I remember thinking to myself the necessity of remembering the goal of my journey: to meet as many people and experience as many things as possible, to live fully in the ever fleeting moment.

In the grand scheme of my adventure this segment of experience was still so near the beginning; my flight from Honolulu to Los Angeles will be my first time home to see my parents in several months.

I am beginning to enter into a deeper recognition that every individual is so different, and that all people change with time. As we live and grow apart from those people we were once close to they do not always look the same to us at second glance. People's habits and personalities change over time with the experiences they encounter and the ways in which they learn to process stimuli. When returning home for the first time in a while one may notice many changes in the lives of persons they know; changes in their personal lives, relationships, and within societies as a whole. Businesses we once knew, loved and frequented close and new ones open. The roads are worked on, trees cut down and others planted. The politicians change; people move and find new employment, some graduate from their educational facilities while others drop out of school. It can be like stepping back into a familiar world after an extended sleep. One in which you were not actually sleeping, merely living in a different geological environment, and one in which you were changing as well.

The type of life experience I am undergoing and processing has made it abundantly evident that change is eminent, that it is constantly occurring everywhere. This 'problem' of change is something that human consciousness will always have to deal with. Even if one does not return to a place which they once lived, that is to say even if they remain in the same place, or that they never return to some place that they previously lived, they are still susceptible to an ever changing world. This issue as far as my knowledge extends was first addressed thousands of years ago by the great Greek philosopher Heraclitus when he stated that 'There is nothing permanent except change'. This viewpoint of the world seems to assert that we cannot come to absolute conclusions and that we must engage our entire lives trying to cognitively adapt and adjust to the many changes which occur. How to do so is a complicated feat, and will likely be relatively different for each individual, but I suppose some measures can be exacted to remedy the situation; the primary step being extending love and positivity. If our first step is something as beautiful as love and positivity good things eminently will follow.

It is not always easy to be positive about things which we perceive, but this bleakness of our perception serves consciousness no good; bleakness of perception and doubts are things which are stagnant of a positive intentionality towards change, it slows our expanding evolution as independent beings. If we continue to treat stimuli which first displeased us as if it is eternally and absolutely displeasing then it is fated to be such. Moreover, if we want to constantly improve the status of things as our consciousness wraps around them we would be wise to attempt each time we reconsider something to add to it positivity; in doing so we aid its existence with the addition of our own positive energy, rather than to endowing upon it a surplus of even more bad energy. If we truly will things to change, and not only will but apply that will in the fullest extent that we are able then we should find how great our influence can be on the state of things, and how accepting we can be of change.

The Streets of Los Angeles

May 16

I left Los Angeles International Airport and went to downtown LA to a bar off of 7ᵗʰ and Figueroa with my good friends Alex Emmerson and Joshua Lupien. The first bar we attempted to go to was the famous Whiskey Bar, which would not allow me in because I was wearing shorts and slippers. Oops, I had become too comfortable in Hawaiian attire for them. I had forgotten to adapt my attire for the switch in geographic location and cultural normality. We decided to walk to another bar without such degrading social standards imposed such as strict dress codes. It was great catching up with my good old friends Alex and Josh, whom with I shared a great deal of my youth and adolescence. We left the bar and were headed back towards the car, surrounded by concrete and metal in the streets of Los Angles. I found myself gazing up at a sky filled with sky scrapers, smog, and light pollution. Josh was on route towards his hotel room as his little sister was graduating from the University of Southern California the next day; his hotel was on the way towards Alex's car, so we all walked together for some time.

During this walk we were approached by a man with a rag and a bucket. He was not drunk nor did he appear to be under the influence of any drugs as Los Angeles prejudices would warn. His name was Barry and he wanted to know if we wanted to have the car window washed. I told him I personally had no car and couldn't help as I had no cash on me. I did commend him however, as many persons do far less honest things to get by in the world. And that if he continues doing what is right he will find a way to get by. To which he replied, "Conversations are worth something". And he walked off across the street in search of someone who was in need of his services. I recall my marvel as I was thinking at that moment that this was such an incredibly deep statement given by Barry, he is in his own right a philosopher.

The preconceptions we might have towards someone are just that attempts at judging before having adequate knowledge. In practical action this is our imaginations at work trying to protect us, in that we cannot help but to hold suspicion towards things which we feel are possibly threatening and towards which we hold uncertainty. I assert that even those things which cause us to be uneasy can be aided by positivity. A few words of encouragement rather than defamation or ignoring ones' humanity are blessings we may bestow upon the world. Perhaps the kind thing you say to someone is the first kind thing they have heard in a very long time. What a terrible world it would be to live in if we never were to hear kind things about ourselves or to never speak kind words to others whom which we come in contact with. That would certainly not be the kind of world I want to live in, so I try to do what I can every day to confront these issues, and to add what positivity I can muster up to offer the world. As difficult as it may be at times and at times it can be really difficult.

Prevalence of Humor

No matter where we are raised, what our language is, our race, gender, or our occupation humor functions as a means to the ends of receiving pleasure. Appreciating humor and the subsequent act of laughing makes us physically feel good. Laughing overwhelms the laugher with a protruding orbital sphere of positive energy. Because humans have a drive towards pleasure we tend to seek out things which fulfill the drive and develop preferences towards humor is a healthy means of fulfilling this drive. This tendency towards humor preference helps us to unwind and relax in the tenseness of human situations. The stresses of uncertainty can be obliterated when laughter and a humorous understanding is applied to the stressful stimuli. The action of laughter itself emits resignations of positive energy; that positivity then reverberates and spreads. The positivity is rooted in the laugher and extends outwards affecting the immediate environment. The alleviation that humor provides then is a key to unlocking peace amidst the weirdness and awkwardness of conscious existence.

Interactions with strangers can often cause anxiety. The unknowingness of the person, their personality, and what their energy frequencies are like can cause consciousness to linger into the realm of malaise. However, through adjusting consciousness with willful positive intent there is relief which can be habitually accumulated! Shedding a smile is a fantastic way to prepare any interaction for excellence. In keeping with allowing openness to new experiences I find a smile and its emphasis on positivity at the forefront of pragmatic intentionality. And so slowly but surely humor finds its way into the fabric of the weirdness of life, thusly it offers not only existential relief but also encourages a positive environmental out-pact.

What magic humor is in the fortification of relationships and cooperative existence? Sharing a laugh is a physical outbound expression of received enjoyment of a conscious experience. When the laugh is not only noted, but acknowledge and returned by another or group of others this sharing solidifies the emotional connections between individuals. Humor then, when used as a tool strengthens consciousness and collective consciousness. What benefits it can provide when instead of one internally collapsing at the sight of a stress inducing stimuli we choose instead to mentally conquer the occurrence with a laugh. Once humans accept this methodology of treating our existential malaise with humor we can work at reducing the stress of our overall predicaments when we train ourselves to react in this light mode of perception, a light mode which can lift into a happy state. And furthermore, not only a happy state but a state which once induced can transcend the barriers of communication as it does not require technical definitions or language to be transmutable to other conscious entities.

Humor is not limited to linguistics and the telling of jokes. It encompasses as well the viewing of images, direct experience witnessing through sensual capacities, the audio reception of a funny sound (such as a fart), or anything that tickles our consciousness and brings to it a positive hormonal secretion and thusly consciously alleviating the pains of our existential conditions. In conclusion of the argument for humor if we choose what to laugh at, and when to laugh, and to choose laughing often we can allow ourselves into certain flux patterns of thought-space in which our cognitive effectiveness can flourish.

Back to the Garden

May 17

In regards to those friends in life which are like family, when time and distance are no longer separated it is a joyous occasion indeed. You will know and love them your whole life through. So come sit down with them and do the things which friends who have not seen each other in a long time do and celebrate!

Humans all come from somewhere. That is that we all have a home town, parents whose genetic combination resulted in us, we all have histories and memories. What we attach to in our world defines us as humans and fundamentally shapes our baseline operating habits. Our identities evolve as we expand our consciousness, and are largely impacted by our environment and those whom exist within and shape our environment in our earliest years. I am speaking of those human experiences so primal to our identity that we no longer even remember them; they morphed into our personal constitutive basis of being. They shaped us and our moral fibers into exactly what we are today.

Family

May 17

Family may not always be stable, but it is enduring. Family is a bond of spirits which runs far too deep for life to be able to shatter. Sometimes family drifts away, sometimes communication stops, we may not even see each other again in life, but still the spirit is related in unchangeable ways.

True love is eternal,
It is strong,
It is wild,
It will survive even after life ends.

You may feel that this runs in contest with the statement earlier in the book that 'nothing in life is constant except change'. Only I suggest love does change; it shifts forms, varies in amounts given and received, and it experiences frequency intensity fluctuations. As it grows and shrinks, we generally say that it is true love if it has a timeless aspect to it. It defies its own diminishing because it is strong enough to always will itself into existence. This is the kind of love families share, persons share with long term lovers and soul mates, as well as the kind lifelong friends share. This love is a type of love which can never be fully extinguished yet as I argued it is still a concept which like all things is constantly subject to change.

Mountain Biking

May 21

It is good for the mind to get out of the city from time to time, and balance modern city life with the beauty of nature. The wide open spaces and flourishing of life provide conscious streams with the openness and ambiguity that is needed to activate imagination. Besides I find it incredibly worthwhile to seek out aesthetic enjoyment from natural scenes of life flourishing. Generally and perhaps ignorantly speaking the people whom inhabit California are much less friendly than they are in Hawaii, the social compaction I feel here is making it difficult to feel free. In the context of a negative energy environment we are so often forced to remediate the negative energies being asserted upon us from societal competition. People seem to really not want to be bothered; they do not want to connect with their fellow man, or so I think.

It was a beautiful day, and despite the Southern Californian smog you could see for miles off over the toll roads and into the raw nature of the canyons. After riding the trail loops around the watershed I found myself atop a hill at Peter's Canyon. I took a break here to catch my breath, at least what I consider to be taking a break... and began to roll a cigarette before bombing down the other side of the hill.

As I was sparking up a man approached me and said, "I hate these hills, they are the worst part", to which I replied, "This is the best part... the view!" His name was Wilber, he had the courage to reach out to a fellow human being, and though I would much have appreciated the preface to a conversation be positive, I recognized his attempt at connection and tried to offer him in return what positivity I had available. Indeed after I had stated this he agreed, thanked me for the perspective the conversation provided him with, and staggering off in newfound method of contemplation he left the area by the bench and glared out across the lake and surrounding hills.

Going North

May 26

My father, sister and I set off on a road trip north to Sacramento for my cousin Julie's wedding, and to see the family we had not seen in 10 years, since the funeral of my grandfather Don's first wife. We drove up route 395 which goes through the high desert into the eastern side of the Sierra Nevada Mountains. We first stopped at Manzanar, a former site of a Japanese internment camp during World War II.

When I was studying in high school at Magnolia Lyceum I had a chance to read a novel written by a young girl who was an inmate at Manzanar during the 1940's titled, 'Farewell to Manzanar'. I remember how terrible it had made me feel that we Americans could be such hypocrites at times, fighting 'fascism' for so many years while enforcing fascist policies on our own soils.

We then took the short drive north to Bishop, California for lunch where we ate at the famous Erik Schat's bakery, the original home of sheepherders' bread, which of course I ordered my sandwich to be made with. We ate our lunch sitting on the patio outside of the restaurant. I almost always prefer outdoor seating. Bishop was an interesting town full of passer-byers, donkey and mule enthusiasts, and ranchers.

From there we admired the beautiful scenery all the way up the eastern Sierra's until we arrived at Mono Lake. Which rests in a volcanic crater, home to two small volcanos which sit in the lake, and another volcano is located at the side, just off Mono Lake. This Volcano off to the side has a rim and a cap in the crater, which is an interesting sight to see. None of the volcanos I have seen in Hawaii are quite like this trio. We drove out to it and hiked. Well they hiked part of the way, and I chose to jog the entirety of the rim. At a few thousand feet in elevation, I ran out of breath and grew dizzy. It was well worth the extra effort for the view.

We took a road I had surveyed from the far northern point of the volcano's rim to the south tufas of the lake. The lake has no outlets so tufas develop there. Tufas are carbonized calcium deposits which grow upwards from the lake into impressive natural mineral formations, which are very fragile. They looked so remarkably majestic protruding from the surface of the lake.

We then carried on to check out the visitor center which was already closed for the day, and checked into our room at the Lake View Lodge. We walked from the room up the street of the small town to Bodie Mike's, a BBQ restaurant where I ordered a rack of ribs; it had been so long, too long since I had had ribs. The next morning we had breakfast at the dinner next door. I ordered a huge cinnamon roll and fresh fruit. I often have thought that small towns with privately owned establishments have some the best food. Then we drove up to Bodie town, which is an old ghost town which used to be a gold mine Mecca.

There after we briefly toured South Lake Tahoe after driving through the south of Carson City, Nevada and Minden. Eventually we arrived in Sacramento. My father and I stayed the night at an inn in Rancho Cordova after we dropped my sister Emilie off at University of California Davis where she stayed with a friend. Upon entering the room my father found a cricket on the pillow, he immediately ran back to the front desk to request a room change. I would have happily picked up the cricket and placed it outside myself had I had the chance.

When we are growing up we often take for granted the presence of our family members, they are always with us loving us and supporting us through our young lives. For some there comes a time as an adult when we take off from our lives and try to make it whether in a relationship, or on our own. We may not have what it takes at first. We will face some of the hardest challenges during our young lives at this time. We will make mistakes and we will learn from our mistakes, each day growing stronger and more independent into the future. We will also face those long uncomfortable days and nights where we wish for nothing more than to be surrounded in such a hearth of love. When the days are long and the work is hard it can be rough to make it out there without your family. So those moments when you get the chance to return, and when you get to feel that for even a small while, you cherish so much more. From mom's homemade dinners, talks with your little brother, that beer or glass of wine you share with your father, or when you look at your sister and realize just how much she has grown and how strong she has become over the years. As uncomfortable as it may be at first to come home, or as hard and emotionally draining as it may be to leave, this is a wonderful human experience to love people in the way that a family once disconnected loves each other when reunited.

Sometimes year's even decades may build up without seeing your family in person, but when you see them again you can feel it in the air, that type of love particular to persons of the same blood, of the same stock, with a common ancestor and a future together as a family. You find the deep pockets of history, about where you come from that you were not previously aware of. You find stories, bonds, and in the meantime they help you to find yourself. There are those moments when relatives get to be together which are some of the most comfortable moments we will ever have, being with people with whom we have no fear because there is a love stronger than any fear which lies at the basis of a family. .

Catching Up

June 17

The summer since my last entry has been a blur, even now as I sit and write my mind wanders through Sutter's Mill and Auburn, past the river fork and across the golden gate bridge, into the park and into the city of San Francisco; then to Big Sur and down the windy coast of California, Los Angeles and to the original Tommy Burger with my father, eventually returning to North Tustin, and then going onwards to Los Vegas.

I spent some time in an area of Newport Beach called Corona Del Mar in a beautiful house two blocks away from the sea. There I played Frisbee with my friend Adam. While we were playing at the park some children requested to play with us. They left a rather humorous impression on me as although Adam is some 6 years my elder the children asked us if I was Adam's dad. We both laughed at the innocence and wonder of the children.

I am forcing guilt upon myself for the fact that I have not been more diligent in writing this journal. I am at the moment unsure if life has meaning or if it is a random matrix of existence primordial to thought and meaning. I leave for Europe in a week, there is so much left to do to prepare for my adventure. Hello Sarte books. Bon Soiree!

Part Three

LE DEPART
POUR EUROPE

A l'Air

24 Juin

I am in the air on a seventeen hour direct flight from Los Angeles International Airport to Charles de Gaulle, to pass the time I read.

How nerve wrecking it is to leave the country especially by one's self for the first time; to put yourself in awkward situations and to enjoy and learn about new cultures. At the end of all the fears you could possibly imagine and conjure up lies the real beauty of new experiences- new experiences which are waiting to reveal themselves to anyone who has the courage to seek them out. One must first face their fears in order to conquer their fears. How do we find the motivation to be courageous?

Are we running from things in our past or are we running towards things in the future when we take these leaps in our lives? Perhaps we are doing both, running away from the things we want to change and in transferring that energy we are pulling away from the past and using it as our motivation, forcing its velocity into our futures. In overcoming these fears we find liberty, and we experience enjoyment and fulfillment in our lives. The satisfaction comes from witnessing these dreams we dare courageously to dream coming true. When your dreams come true, I hope you are really able to cherish the moment, it may disappear from you as quickly as it had arrived.

Perdu á Paris

26 Juin

From looking around and observing my environment empirically, I have decided that everyone here is lost. It is not just me. Though I have not yet figured out the 'why' in the statement that everyone is lost. It is however an intriguing and interesting experience for me to stand here and watch the passersby. Watching may be the best way to be lost, just resting and observing. Not forcing the consciousness to be in any hurry to find oneself. At first I thought that I was lost because I did not know my way around, yet I felt as though many Parisians seemed to be just as lost in the business and confusion of life in a large city.

You can notice how lost we humans are in our lives when shuffling around busy airports, seeing the stress and the anxiety of all these persons trying to solve the little puzzles of their day. They all have the dream or the idea of where they are going and can imagine what they think is their actual destination. Yet, when you look more closely you notice that all humans are lost in route, all of us are distracted and get confused on our course to wherever it is that we think we are going. We might have this general aim or goal of what we are going to do and where we are going to go but we must constantly adjust in life to all the things we cannot control, all the things we could not have possibly known were going to be factors when we were dreaming up our dreams.

It reminds me of watching bees searching for pollen, the bee sets out from the hive with this quest. Yet during his search (yes bees who leave the hive are in fact all male sex bees), he finds himself distracted by colors, objects, and beings. He sometimes investigates humans with such an awkward curiosity. Most people do not care for it when a bee begins to hover around them, but before long they usually take off and return to their search or pollen. After all, this is what he must do, it is in his nature. How could a bee be any more than a bee could be anyways?

I met a Parisian man named Oliver right away out-side of Charles De Gaulle Airport. I lit his cigarette for him and asked him how to get to Gare du Nord. He informed me that he was going the same way and he helped me to get tickets and find my way. He was

42 years old and lives half in Montreal, Canada and the rest of the time in Paris, France. He called himself a dinosaur as he has no phone, email, or internet. I find that Oliver is a very friendly, helpful, liberal, and happy person. After figuring out trains for the next for days at Gare du Nord I took the number 5 metro to La République and dropped off my bags at my hostel.

Perhaps if an individual is able to be conscious enough to notice how lost they are, they can better recognize that everyone else around them is lost. I like to think that at least some of the people around me know at least a segment or two of the way. Connecting with them is a crucial step in accessing their potential knowledge. If you accentuate kindness and display it even to unlikely characters you will find connections easier to forge. Furthermore, you never know who along your path to your imagined destination is able to help you.

In further reflection I think of how good it feels to help others, and it should be instilled in the character of a person with 'good morals' to try to help others whenever possible. Do we not in establishing these connections also benefit from knowing how to accept the kindnesses which we receive from others? This exchange of respect for the other humans around us is essential to community, not only the offering of your services but knowing how to receive and to reemit other persons' kindnesses. If you had an entire theoretic town that was constantly reflecting each other's kindness I think you would find yourself in a rather pleasant and kind community.

Our fear of others and our fears of ourselves being judged are what keep these shockwaves of kindness from commencing and or continuing. We can be so terrified of satisfying these imaginary external societal expectations that we often forget those expectations which we have of ourselves, of what we have determined our roles should be, and if we are not true to ourselves I imagine it will be hard for anyone else to be true to us either.

Having just arrived at my hostel I was trying to figure out how to connect to the internet on my phone so that I could contact my friend Kiersten from Hawaii whom has been living in Paris for the past six months. I was trying to figure out the conflabbit device when Keirsten poked her head inside the door of the hostel and said, "Bonjour Dan". I was shocked to hear my name but so grateful to see a familiar face and to have a guide for the day in Paris, Her friend Chris who studied with her in Paris and also studies at the University of Hawaii joined us as well. With that we were off, we road bikes and got Indian food, road all over Paris and went to Notre Dame! We then bought a bottle of wine and drank it along the Seine. When we were done we wrote a note, placed the note in the bottle, corked it and sent it on its way down the river. Shortly after Kiersten had to catch a flight to Chicago and we parted ways.

Now that my friends had left and I was once more on my own I went back to Gare du Nord to fix a train issue, and decided to wander and get lost in Paris. I sat on a bench near Arc de Triomphé and watched the madness in the traffic circle. I was only further convincing myself of my theory that everyone really was lost. How could we ever really know where we are, or where we are going? There I met Astrid a French girl, she told me she was scared, nervous and anxious about her future. She was certainly lost in the big city and in life in the more broad sense, ironically just like everyone else I had seen that day. Perhaps I had been incorrect about the lost-ness' of others. Maybe I was displacing and extending my own feelings of being lost onto others. We talked for some time, then I left. Even though I sensed she didn't want me to go something in her eyes and the way she held my hand for so long told me so. Maybe it was due to the sparseness of human connection in such a large city. I knew she was clinging onto something; we all are clinging onto things from our pasts. I went right back to getting lost, by myself.

Eventually I found the Eiffel Tower! Just before sunset where I met a young woman named Chelsea and her mom, they were from Oregon/ Texas. They were really nice and we talked for a while about life, cultural differences in different areas of the United States, about their experiences traveling in Europe, education, etc. Also sitting nearby was a French girl and her German friend. They were very nice as well. I walked with them through the city for a while and we all gawked at the Parisian architecture and the grandeur of design in the well-lit city. In my opinion thus far Paris is much more beautiful at night than during the day.

It is amazing the kinds of people you can meet traveling, the things you can learn and how interesting a conversation with complete strangers can be, that is if you can get over the fear of them being 'strangers'. I recall from childhood I must have heard hundreds of times not to trust strangers, but in fact strangers have taught me many lessons. I learned how to ride a bike after trying to learn from my own father many times; finally it was a complete stranger at my neighbor and family friend's garage sale who helped me conquer balancing. I learned how to play guitar, and how not to judge people from a man named Tony who was at first a stranger, but in time we became great friends. I was told by my parents to judge him for his long hair and tattoos. What horrible advice that turned out to be, I am glad I didn't listen to the voices of society echoing through my parents mouths and did instead what I knew was right by befriending him.

Or even for example Oliver the man I met at the airport in France was of wondrous help, but not a person that you would likely expect a young man like myself to converse with. Each of these people who in their own relative ways had changed my life were strangers to whom I extended a great deal of human respect and who returned that respect by enriching my life. You will never know until you know, and even then it's debatable. So live and find out in the meantime.

26 Juin

To think and to contain those thoughts solely within ones' own mind is not enough. To speak without following through is insufficient. To both write and to read is helpful in self-advancement. But to really move one must move, and to live one must live! Fear is the great immobilizer; it disintegrates possibility moment by moment. Destroy fear.

27 Juin

My friend Gryphn and I came up with the question every traveler should ask: What is in your pocket in Amsterdam? I realized that I did not know what was in my pocket! Things, stuff, hands, air? What did any of that really mean anyways?

I was amazed upon my arrival in Europe that so many of my preconceptions were completely wrong. It was time to change my mentality on all the things which I thought I knew and to allow myself to be open to new experiences. On the train as languages began to shift I did the best I could to mentally prepare myself for shifts in my understanding of the world, my understanding of humanity, and my understanding of my own place in existence.

I had an interesting train ride; it was beautiful to see the countries and cities draped in green rolling hills and buildings still standing after centuries. We have nothing of this age in the United States. I met people in the lounge of my hostel and before I knew it I was running around the old red brick streets which line the canals of Amsterdam. We stopped to eat sandwiches before visiting a coffee shop. Such liberality and so many people responsibly acting upon their civil liberty is a really beautiful thing to see in a society. The Netherlands is certainly a leader in the world in terms of making a comfortable and non-oppressive society for their citizens to live within. I then went with my new friend Gryphn from Boston and a Canadian couple from Montreal who were all staying in my hostel to the Heineken Brewery. After the brewery tour we took

*the brewery's boat and got a tour of a few of the canals.
It was awesome. I was particularly amused that there
were so many house boats along the canals!*

*What an interesting way to create a habitude! The
house boats were all connected to sewer and electric
lines, and the interiors were fitted to look much more
similar to a house than that of the interior of a boat.
These are a real marvel of the cities innovation. I am
trying to process all the interesting insights into the
nature of human ingenuity I am experiencing in this
country; a country which is largely comprised of land
reclaimed by the sea in a feat of incredible engineering.*

*Which do way do you face oh masters of the human
race? With young faces and tongues, tobacco stained
lungs. Do you believe half as much as you perceive
or is it yourself and not the others which you deceive?*

I think we lie to ourselves all the time, I think we lie to
ourselves because we think we are protecting ourselves from
our fears and the dangers of truth. We lie to make ourselves
more comfortable with situations that we face in life. Does
not this dishonesty cause us confusion? We trick ourselves
from that which actually occurs to that which we want to
have occurred because we often only allow what is beneficial
to us to remain in our memories. Are we not stained by these
internal workings of the human subconscious? We only are
allowed access to the surface of our minds actual functioning. Do we really believe half of what we think we see, or are
we making up a great deal of these things which we consti-
tute into reality? To ask again in different words- Are we just

fooling ourselves for our own benefit? Do we really live a life in which we are afraid to be honest with ourselves? Maybe at times we live in self-honesty, but maybe like most things this varies given the particular instance, the individual, and the environment in which they operate.

So far my perception of the Dutch people is that they are a very humorous people with a peculiar sounding language. It only sounds funny to me of course because I am not personally used to hearing it. That night I met an Italian couple who was staying in my room at the hostel, Claudia and Simone. They live in Amsterdam and go to school here, their dormitory housing contract at the university had expired and it would be a week still until they were able to get their new apartment for the summer and upcoming semester. I woke up to them packing their things to leave the hostel very early in the morning. After they left I woke up as well and headed downstairs for a cigarette. Down on the street outside the door I saw Simone. He said he had work in an hour and a half but was wondering if I had any plans for the day. I told him that I did not, but that I wanted to get breakfast. And so he took me to go and eat with him at the café where Claudia works. He was a really good hearted person; I could feel it in his vibes. It was really nice to have breakfast with an Amsterdam local.

Afterwards I met Gryphn back in the lounge of the hostel where we had agreed to meet. We met up and began walking towards the Van Gogh museum. Walking along the old canals was quite a trip! There are so many small windy roads and confusing street names which always threw me off. When we got inside the museum I was astounded by the paintings which I had seen so many times in photographs now real, vibrant, and textured right before my very eyes. I fell so overwhelmed it was as though I had fallen in love with the paintings one by one as I viewed them.

As my time at the museum went on I was irked more and more so by the tourists who were in attendance at the museum that day, mainly the type who would walk from painting to painting, frame up with a camera or a phone a perfectly framed picture of the painting, capture the image and move along, with hardly any thought as to the real substance of the artwork; caring only for its surface aesthetics and presumably as well only to be able to say that they had indeed seen it, without attempting or even contemplating the attempt to understand. I could hardly take so much of this. Eventually when I was staring at a rather well known painting of Van Gogh's, Carrefour et Citrons, I felt compelled to do something about it. I had been staring at the painting for some time, trying to figure it out in all its complex simplicity, when a young British girl, about 12 years old, approached the painting. I do not know where it came from but she produced and iPhone and wandered towards the painting, blocking my view. I looked at the screen and sure enough she had sized up what she considered a perfect image of the painting, clicked capture and began to walk away.

I stopped her; I asked her if she minded if I asked her a question regarding the painting, she replied that this would be alright. I asked her, "why do you think he spent so much time painting something so simple as a carrefour and lemons?" to which she humbly replied, "I do not know", then she ran away in some odd and confused shame for not having produced a more suffi-cient answer to the question.

Yet I had received exactly the reaction I had hoped for. I did not think she would have at that point had a real good conception of why he painted it, but what I had hoped for was for her to think. My intention in this experiment being that hopefully the next painting that she inspects, rather than just capturing an image she will take a moment to really reflect herself against the painting; to really soak in all the vibrancy, all that the painter is trying to suggest with each and every brush stroke, and to take the concepts that she relates to it and make them her own.

What kind of existence would this be, to live and live and to not think, to not reflect, to not take those precious moments which we experience and make them our own? In doing so would we not dis-allow ourselves from painting around us our very own dreams and wishes? We may be fearful to be so liberated, as to think that we can actually influence life, to not just be washed over by the harsh waves of existence, but to paint a beach to our own liking; and then to walk down onto this perfectly painted beach, sit down and enjoy a day of our very own creating, to our very own liking. Life intends to scare us, society wishes to expose to us those most frightening aspects of the human endeavor, so that we might run to it. Pitiful and desperate we are expected to cling to society, to express greatly and often our need for society.

Is not this status of being like living without ever noticing that you are alive? To walk about through life, aware that it is, but without ever having any conception as to the implications that follow this awareness. What a shame, there must be more; I thirst for it, for a deeper point, a deeper purpose. I honestly feel as if I cannot walk about just doing what I expect is expected of me all of the time. I must try to experiment and to examine things, to relate to them, to make my ideas off of them and to make those ideas my own, because I can.

28 Juin

Walking around Amsterdam was fun, Derrick and I went on a mission for our last night to take pictures at the I Amsterdam sign. It was lovely to walk around in such great weather, as the rain had just ceased before we departed. After completing our mission we parted ways. He returned to the hostel and I went to walk around the city a bit more on my last night, I eventually returned to the hostel.

Irish girls were yelling in the hallway at the base of the stairs that they were having trouble getting into their room. I met them on the stairs. After trying to console them and informing them that the front desk would not be open again for another 6 hours at 9 am, and that the best advice I could offer is to continue trying the room key until the door finally works, and opens.

They thanked me for my help and I took off up the 4 impossible flights of stairs to my room to finish packing and get some sleep before taking a train back to France.

As I got near my door, they exclaimed, "He is the bloke that is in our room!!" Yes indeed it was I who was to share the room with them that night but I had no clue that this was the case when I met them in the hallway. I let them into the room and as I began to pack, they began to talk. One of the Irish girls was quite batty. She told me at first that I was gorgeous, and commented on my eyes. But was quite immature and thought it would be fun to tease me. Eventually I told her off, she laughed and loved it. This Irish girl was so weird. Finally the sun had risen; my train was in an hour so I wished them a good stay in Amsterdam and took off on foot for the train station.

When I got to the train station I could not find my lighter. So I went into the store to purchase one when an American tourist heard me ask for a lighter he turned to me and said, "Here is a lighter. I do not smoke back home and no longer need this, I am about to get on a plane, take it. It's yours." I was stunned at the kind gesture took from him lighter and walked back out onto the streets of Amsterdam to smoke one last cigarette before leaving the city of liberty.

Finally I am on a train to Lyon, I almost did not make it in time. The seats were already completely full. I stopped in the compartment near the doors and the lavatory and sat on my bag leaning up against the wall for a least an hour. During the time I was sitting there waiting for a seat to open up a weird French guy took a seat on the toilet seat and was yelling the whole time. It made me feel very uncomfortable! At some point a man had left the seating compartment to use the lavatory. The man on the phone who was sitting on the toilet yelled at him to piss off. He told him the bathroom was occupied. Frightened, the man left and went off presumably to search for another lavatory elsewhere on the train.

Eventually I was able to get a seat and finally relax with my belongings feeling safe. After leaving such a peaceful country as the Netherlands I feel like there are some sketchy characters here in France. International tensions are high at this moment in human history. Edward Snowden had just revealed that the US government was spying upon the citizens of European ally nations through their internet and phone communications. I felt as though it was not a comfortable time to be an American traveling abroad, but that so long as I don't speak and English I think I will be okay.

I looked up for a second from this book I am writing in and this pretty French girl is staring at me with a very intense glare. I asked her where on the map we were. She was confused by my accent, and she asked me where I was from. She found out I was American and immediately switched from talking in French to English; my guise had failed as soon as I opened my mouth. She is a dancer, more precisely a ballerina and was on the train from her home in Normandy, on route to the South of France for the weekend. She shared with me some of her French music she was listening to on her iPod.

I suppose this is life in France, I am finding it true what is said about the women here being so much more cultured and mature than the American girls I know; they are so determined and certain of themselves, a confidence rarely found in girls raised in my culture. I think this is an aspect of the culture I am really enjoying here in France. I was slightly disappointed to find eventually that this beautiful dancer was only 16 years old; I would have guessed her to have been 20. In America things are far different than they are in France, I would be shunned for talking to so young a girl even as casually as we were speaking to each other. Life after all should be a grand adventure, but often cultural normalities are strong at play.

One facet of my culture which I very much dislike but still find myself prone to being guilty of myself is being overly judgmental of other human beings. I feel that in the United States we are taught to judge everyone and everything. Even if the second later I realize that I am being judgmental and try to counteract it, it is often times too late and the possibility for effective communication with that individual has been blocked by some bad energy transference which was completely unconscious and incidental. What can we do about such things, such things which are culturally engrained into us run so deep into our methods for handling events in our lives? I would in earnest like to hope and believe that we can overcome this and we can retrain ourselves to make our reactions to prejudice loaded stimuli different and more loving. Even if it is a farfetched dream, in this uncomfortable life we have created for ourselves through our social constitutions I would like to at very least be allowed to be free from these oppressions in my dreams, if I am so able.

28 Juin

No sleep. It is 23h and I am at the train station in Lyon Part Dieu. I smoked a lot of cigarettes while I waited, waited and waited more. On the way from Paris to Lyon, while I was listening to the French girls' music, the train had to stop for some fifteen minutes because something was on the tracks. When I had arrived in Lyon my train was late and I missed the last train of the day to Annecy. I had booked a room at the Annecy hostel so that I could sleep there that night and at 9h the next day I was to meet my French host family whom I was to live with for the next five weeks while I study French. The first train the next day to Annecy is in eight hours, at 7h the next morning. I do not know what I am going to do to pass the time. I feel as though I am very lost, and after a long day of traveling I am so tired. Hardly any of the people here in Lyon speak English, only French and my French at the moment is not very fluent. I feel that it is good for me though, because I really am benefiting form being forced to practicing using my French and not use my English. I think that my mind at current is working far more slowly than usual. I do not know anymore. I am certainly lost. I need sleep.

I am waiting here outside the train station, in a small garden near the bus station, drinking water, writing, reviewing my photos from Amsterdam and Paris. Amsterdam was such a fun experience but I think I prefer to be in France, at least for now. The town Lyon and the people who live here are very bizarre to me, but I am learning to love the awkwardness of the experience. Everything is new to see, the expansions of my understanding of life and all its difference and complexity is good for me, and is certainly helping me to grow as a person, and as a thinker... as a Philosopher.

I was approached by quite a few men while I was at the train station they tried to pick me up, but I was disinterested. At about 1 am, I really wanted to brush my teeth, the train station was closed, and so was most of the town. I took out my toothbrush and bottle of water and sitting in the garden adjacent to the bus station I began to brush my teeth. I noticed a man who was sitting on another bench in the garden looking at me as if I was indeed quite bizarre myself. I was so bored that I decided when I was done I would go and talk to him, because I really needed something to do to occupy my time. I had not slept much in the past few days and needed something to help keep me awake. His name is Dominique and he informed me that all the cafes were already closed because it was so late, but that he would not mind allowing me to come to his house and to drink coffee there so I could stay awake for my journey.

He was clearly not interested in the company of women, but he was a gentleman and just wanted to help out a stranger who was passing through his town, which I greatly appreciated. We went back to his place which was right near the train station, he stood in the kitchen and I sat on a chair on the other side of the kitchen's bar. He made me as much coffee as I asked for and we spoke much of the politics of our two nations, and of philosophy as well, particularly discussing the philosophy of French existentialism. I told him that I was not gay but that we could be friends on an intellectual level. He helped me improve my French a great deal. It was actually I who made things awkward sexually between us and entirely on accident. I asked before leaving if he could go onto Google and print me out a map of the city so that I could go and check out the river Seine before returning to the train station.

I was not facing towards the computer as he turned it on, but eventually I turned around facing into his living room, and saw the background image of his desktop computer, which was of two men in their late twenties standing naked in a garden peeing. He was highly embarrassed and I told him not to be as he was not expecting a visitor and that it was his house and his computer and he had a right to do what he would like to in his own home. I took the map and left.

When I got back to the train station, I met a really cool guy from Vein; he spoke some English because he is a rapper and has learned English through listening to American rap songs. We spoke a great deal of fusing different languages together in music to convey a single solitary message. His name was Joe. The people here are becoming to appear more hospitable the better I get to know them and the more of them that I meet; they are all very surprised to meet an American, particularly one who speaks French, even if I do so poorly. I am so glad for humanity and philosophy that this is how the world is; that people are people through and through, that there can be so much humanity and positivity amongst strangers and people from different countries. It really feels good at the moment to be in a world like this! La vie est belle! I still need sleep.

An Essay on Human Dignity

Each person from their own individual perspective is the center of their own world. All their thoughts and ideas are primarily shaped by their memories, experiences, culture, and exposure. This separates them from all other existent conscious individuals. We attempt with great zeal to convey our opinions and our ideas but ultimately we are barricaded into our own existential dilemma. Yet, no one other person can fully understand the thoughts and feelings of any other. We love each other and cooperate to ensure not only our own survival but the survival of our social groups as well, yet we can never completely understand anyone. Every other person will always see things differently, have different emotions evoked by different stimuli, and logically concoct their own methodologies for dealing with situations, and also create their own unique memories as well to events which have occurred based of their experiential biases.

Humans also habitually seek validation of their own existence and their conscious play within their existence. This is the drive towards dignity, explained in a different light it is a drive towards having social expressions of individuality which springs with honesty from one's own internal conscious stream of awareness recognized as valid by others with which they interact. Yet we cannot all always be correct, thusly we often feel as though our dignity is being compromised. We can however attempt to take steps towards improving our own incommunicability. I would like to associate here positivity with goodness. Theoretically in this sense of progressive consciousness when positive energy is asserted, the logical resulting consequence should be goodness, perhaps still a step away from idealized perfection but the best attempt nonetheless. It is a choice to cave into negative sentiments and to allow the negative associations and reactions to govern assertions of will.

Also, if we reflect on the difficulties of ourselves being understood we catch a glimpse into the plight of all humans. In this plight each is as anxious and desperate to feel validated and dignified as a person. Respect for others opinions and perspectives is not always easy to maintain. As new occurrences alter our memories of certain persons we develop bias towards them and towards the methodologies we create for dealing with interactions involving them. This closes our mind to the newness of each moment; in this cognitive barricading we inevitably forsake opportunities and beautiful moments as we assume the modes of reaction that those whom we 'know' will undergo in future events. In a return to prefuture idealism the focus takes one away from the negative doubts of future occurrences and back into self-alignment with the vibratory frequencies emitted from their immediate existences. Perhaps rightful and dignified action within the context of the pre-future requires less thought than we have previously extended as a solution to our woes. We as a survived animal species clearly have made it through harder endeavors than the ones we may face in our current lifetimes. It was our animal programming not our theoretical propositions which saw our species through the vast majority of our history. We are confused by this when we open our history books because thought externalized by linguistics formulates the primary mode of expression in all of our sources. It leads me to ponder what pre-history was like...

One could if they attempted as well gather that as life was immensely different in pre-historical époques- also the face of humanity, government, and society have shifted constantly throughout the course of history. New approaches, ideals and camps of thought have arisen from so many diverse sources that as long as humanity is able to spill itself upon the future newness will continue to arrive. I mention this to fuel the assertion that there will be new systems of interaction, new algorithms which we use to address the problems of human existence. The more positive assertions that are made here in the pre-future the more goodness that will be enacted in the formation of the new forms of thought which will aid us in the future but which have not yet at this time arrived.

Since then we hopefully all wish for our human dignity, and for the pragmatic flourishing in the most good sense of that word for the human species throughout the planet and in the universe as well, we would benefit from putting every first foot forwards in as much positivity as we can muster up. We need not be overdramatic as that can become a public mode of expression which is more accurately a falsification of actual positivity. Nor should we allow ourselves to even become dogmatic about anti-dogmatism. We should be honest in reflection so that our actions are our choices which we make by intelligent willing of certain methods to achieve certain outcomes. Finding a mean in assertion of the virtue of positive optimism should be the root functionality for any individual unit to evolve into a state of positive goodness.

It seems as though there is a pink or purple elephant in the corner of the room and it is staring me straight in the face. The elephant is comprised of the possibility that some individuals are purely self-destructive and rather than relishing the goodness that positivity has to offer they have trained themselves to enjoy the agony and pain of existence. This seems to be the low road. Yet this elephant can easily be poached as these kinds of destructive activity are hardly the actions of a dignified human. Their actions will intrinsically rest invalidated because the methodology of approach is not righteous (or in Hawaiian *Pono*) and causes not only the destruction of the dignity of the individual but also causes those around them harm to their mental and emotional wellbeing.

Any message that begins with anything less than love and positivity is inevitably going to fail the test of goodness. Yet stepping into new and newer still moments of pre-future existentialism we find both the opportunity, and the power to be self-righteous through positive connotation, such that one is always putting forth that which is positive and always attempting to preform acts of positive goodness that they become dignified. That dignity then should translate into social acceptance in a society if that society were good it-self- if that society would respect and be willing to support dignified individuals. I think that this model of action and reaction is best described as being a climate of mutual dignified respect coiled around a positive social centrifuge.

Optimists of humanity should from my perspective band together in support of positive assertions of human consciousness at all times and whenever possible. This is the only rope to which we can trust to cling onto our dignity. It is effectively the thread which holds together the tapestry that is to be our future. It is the element created by our conscious choices in regards to how we interact with the world, and what we through thinking can imaginatively shape it into being. So many will try to discourage the positive and the self-righteous, but we know deep in our hearts when we are deceiving no one, not even ourselves. We can sense our vibrations of spirit and the vibrations of others who assert nothing but the greatest good upon the world and whom expect those reverberations not to administer an immediate reward to the individual conducting positive output, but that the reverberations will reach far beyond the perceptual reaches of that individual. That is when a human really has great reason to feel dignified, to exist in contentment with their own existence. This version of the truly dignified human may be just a dream that dreamers dream today, but without the dream being dreamt it will never have the opportunity to come to fruition.

Temporality Explored

As confusing as life may seem at times, there is always a beauty to be found in the fact that it continues. Though we may be blind at times towards so much of what goes on around us, what other persons are thinking, and the nature of their intentions. We get to wake up every day no matter where we are, and we get to give today another shot, we get to experience and share humanity with those around us at least one more time. As strange as things may get and as depressed as we may at times feel there comes a point in the night when our eyes bring the day to a close, we drift off into our dreams, and we awaken to a new world of possibilities different than any other which has already passed. So long as we cherish and are thankful for our own existences, no matter how much discomfort we feel, we will be able to find immense beauty.

Arriver á Annecy

29 Juin

Finally I arrive in Annecy; I slept a little on the train. Outside of the train station I searched for a taxi, but could not find one. It was early in the morning and not many people were out. I had to get to my schools parking lot in the next 15 minutes, so I decided to take the bus. I got there in perfect timing, my feet literally touching the driveway at 9 a.m. I saw all of the people I knew in my program from Hawai'i, and I met my new host family who I was to live with for the next five weeks. It was nice, and I fell in love with their old French house.

After taking a thirteen hour nap I took a walk down to the Centre Commercial to buy some things which I was going to need during my stay. My first reflections are that Annecy is so beautiful, old, yet well managed. I need to stop writing as I am going to head out to meet up with some of the other students from my program. Goodnight!

After wandering and traveling through so many unfamiliar places, it is reassuring and provides a great sense of stability in life to know that you have a fixed residence, even if it is only temporary. This kind of reassurance in life makes it much easier to have some sense of normalcy. As fun as adventures and new experiences are, we need places and times to reflect on all the changes, and to assess our existence at current after all the recent changes which have occurred. The process of reflection is again highly important, and is necessary if we are to learn anything from our experiences; we have to reevaluate our knowledge continually in order for it to be applicable knowledge.

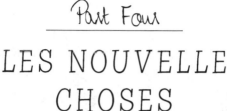

Part Four

LES NOUVELLE CHOSES

First day in Annecy

30 Juin

Today I met with some students from my program. We ate lunch at the beautiful Lac Annecy. Set in the East of France high up in the Alps rests this pristine clear lake. The blueness of the water is vibrant and alluring, the backdrop around this gorgeous body of water are high jagged alps covered in thick alpine forests. Breathtaking! There was a path for a triathlon in part of the town nearest to the lake, we watched for a while cheering on the runners. We hung out at the park near the lake all day, getting familiar with this new and town. Keelan and I live close to each other, so we walked home together.

We should not be surprised if we find life flowing in cycles. There are times of great progress and happiness, times of sadness and a lack of motivation, times at which we feel appreciated, and times we feel that we have no good influence in the world, and times where we feel safe and secure, and times when we feel the world crashing down upon us. If we find ourselves on the low side of a cycle we should rejoice, because once we take the hardest step, we also take our first step on the karmic wheel back to the bright side of things. One should take advantage of their moments to shine, and to utilize their hardest moments to reflect and strengthen themselves.

Annecy

2 Juillet

Annecy is such a quaint little town, full of great people, and certainly spectacular food. I am finding my host family to be extremely helpful in explaining the town and the house to me I should add as well that my host mother is quite the spectacular cook- dinners are made with home grown lettuce for salads and homemade sauce for pasta and pizza- much of which is prepared from the garden at the house.

A few nights ago I walked home with two other students from Hawaii. After dropping our friend off at her at her place, Keelan and I went on our way back to our part of town strolling the dimly lit streets of Annecy when we walked by two French people. A man and a woman, as they passed by, I as a silly exuberant traveler wanting to be friendly to the local people said, "Bon soir!" After they passed I smelled that familiar scent, the sweet smell of smoke. They had a bottle of wine from which they offered me some and I drank, smoked, and talked with them right there on the street where I met them from about 1h until 4h. They were very kind; somehow by the time I left I had arranged some sort of rendezvous in the future with my new friends. Life is beautiful, and very weird.

4 Juillet

I didn't want to waste time traveling from place to place, there was so much to see and I had so much energy billowing out from me- wanting to explore it all. So today I bought a bike. On the previous evening I had met with my friends at the train station, as was becoming usual. Except this time it was raining very hard. She and I looked for a place we could hide and find shelter. A minute or so passed and the man whom I had just met the other day was walking right past me. If I had not met him the night before and acted with friendship towards him, he would have been just another person walking by me on the street that night. Since we had previously met we recognized each other, and we were able to connect again

As big as the world may seem, each region and area has its own limited contents, which undergo frequent interactions with the other contents of the microcosm. Thus one can say this whole big world, is actually con- glomeration of a bunch of very small worlds.

Every day here in France has been beautiful. The lake in particular is stunning. All of the streets and corners of the town are buzzing as the people are preparing for the Tour de France and the national holiday 'Le Quatorze de Juillet'. The vibe of Annecy is shifting around me as summer arrives and with the additional heat the snow was finally disappearing even from the very tops of the Alps. Everyone is in great spirits. I was sitting at a restaurant with my friends enjoying Pizza and enjoying glasses from my first ever bottle of Côtes du Rhône. Amidst the energy of the air in the medieval streets of La Vielle-Ville Annecy I noticed a guy I recognized from school talking to some girls at the cafe across the street. I walked over and talked to him. His name is Bobby Rollof.

Après le 4 Juillet

5 Juillet

At this point I find myself diving deeper into my reflections. Often drifting off on ideas about how beautiful it is to be alive, so young, in good spirits, and with good company. There is some great joy which I find in moments at which I am completely enveloped in the phenomena of feeling alive. It creates an intrigue, a fascination with the realization that I am conscious of my experiences. I enjoy enjoyment, so I have been spending a lot of my time doing what I enjoy most reading, picnicking, swimming and talking with friends and relative strangers along the shores of Lake Annecy.

Bobby somehow had gotten ahold of some Roman Candle fireworks and brought them for us Americans to enjoy. So, I spent this 4th of July sitting on a lake in France, doing something truly culturally American, ironically with my new friend from Amsterdam- Bobby.

After the bar things got crazy. A fight almost broke out between students. Luckily it got dispelled. In lieu of the previous evening's celebrations, class today was hard. I could hardly stay awake or focus having only had two hours of sleep! I made it through the day thanks to my friend Mr. Coffee. Mr. Coffee and I get along great!

The beach at Lake Annecy is different than any other beach I had ever been to. I could sense the dynamic vibe and mix of cultures. Surrounding me were all different kinds of people; Families with children, young men, and beautiful women; some of them topless. There are even old leathery skinned folk, basking in the sun, dreaming of their youth, living in the moment, and waiting patiently to die. Just like the rest of us.

That is exactly what I am doing as well, living in the moment, and waiting patiently to die. All these humans are in the some ways the same and in many ways unique and very different. I am just another of the same different people. But as much as company may be loved, it is as well at times good to be alone.

These seasons of our cycles come and go with so much force. One month you are living a certain lifestyle and another month you have a paradigm shift and no longer do some act any more. You grow in and out of these shells of your own existence. Some people I assume must get comfortable, stuck, or comfortably stuck in certain shells and can remain there for long periods. It is different for every person, and probably changes as well over spans of time. This notion is a large factor as to why I feel it is important to undergo constant reflection of the shells you have grown, the shell you are in, and to idealize and work towards the next shell in your evolutionary wheel. D'où venons-nous? Que sommes-nous? Où allons-nous?

5 Juillet

Sometimes the little insights are what give life some depth.

"Life is either a daring adventure or nothing at all." —Hellen Keller

"My biggest indulgence is thinking, I think too much, or I think when I should act" —Moses Loehr

"There is nothing sexier than intellectual depth" —Moses Loehr

"Forget who you are, what you look like, and be yourself!" —Bobby Rollof

6 Juillet

Nothing in life can be permanent, existence of both thoughts and material form fade. The great philosopher Heraclitus was right in that indeed "one cannot step in the same river twice". I watch as the plants bathe in the light of the sun, brushed gently by the wind and tended to by insects, the fairies of the forest- changing moment by moment temporarily solidifying their existences.

What is it to have anything (i.e to have an opportunity, or an item of possession, love, etc.) anyway? What we may now 'have' in the past we had not, and in the future we likely again will not 'have' it once more. From this logic I think that possessions are a silly thing to grow attachment too. Nothing is eternal and in time, all will fade away into change.

La Buvette du Marchée

7 Juillet

I am currently sitting at the cafe in Annecy with my friend Bobby having a drink. I smoked too many cigarettes as I watched the people parading down the old stone streets for hours. It was highly amusing, and so different from the social vibrations of the places I had come from. I notice each person's unique character, mannerisms, and their apparent oddities. Every face here is new for me. Yet, there is so much more in existence, more than what I can see here from this chair with smoke drifting by in front of my face. Despite the occasional discomfiture and confusion that I sense at times this place offers me a very warm homelike feeling... My mind is getting tired even after café upon café that I drink. Alas I think that soon, we will leave, and I will go home and sleep.

Before I left, Bobby who studies economics said something that really stuck with me, the kind of perspective only Bobby might say, and really mean, when he said;

"In my perfect world there is no money, all basic needs are met. People will not look for a job that makes them money, but would look for a job which they like and then they will meet their full potential." – Bobby Rollof

Without allowing ourselves to fail through trial and error, I am not sure we can ever realize our full potential. Perhaps the changes that are the best to make are the ones which at first seem the most outlandish. It is in the spirit of creativity that newness arises. We take the house of what we know, and renovate it and remodel applying coat after coat of paint, until one day we can sit on the porch of something which we are really satisfied with, admiring something which we created for ourselves.

I really enjoy the time I spend with these people, we so effortlessly blend together our thoughts and our own humanities into a bond of brotherhood, one like which any human can share with another human. Our diverse perspectives when twisted together form a column, an example of how beautiful life can be when we take the time to understand each other. Yet our column is just one of many.

I ponder; if you must sell for a living do you not inadvertently sell your soul as well? How though can we go through life without money and without earning a solid living? One chooses exactly what to focus their attention towards. If you think of negative things and bad situations then that is exactly what you will find. If you think of money problems you will have them, if you think certain things are important you will cause yourself to suffer in pursuit of them regardless of what they are- this is the power that the content of what we focus upon holds over us. In turn, we ultimately determine what it is we wish to focus on. So should we be focused upon money so much that in the pursuit of money we sell ourselves?

The constant mediation of the desires of the individual self and society's expectations of that individual often sets us off and leaves us uneasy, yet our rational self can be its' own lifesaver. It can rescue us from our negative habits; it is by way of consciously *directed thoughts* that we have the most potentiality to heal our wounds and to rethink our positions on life. While it may at times drown us in a sea of unfamiliarity, and discomfort with what we consider normal (our instincts), it as well is the human functionality which allows us to understand the things that were once foreign but which we may through reconsideration make familiar.

8 Juillet

Today was great! I bought a baguette, cheese, and sausage for lunch. The French diet suits me. Class went well, I feel as though I am learning a lot of French and in a very practical sense; even more-so than I felt I was learning in my French courses in Hawaii.

I love coming home to my French family, it is so nice to speak and dine in French. All of my diners are delicious and I get to practice expressing myself and talking about my day, my thoughts, and my feelings in French. It is sweet the way my host mother acts like such a mother and is so understanding of youth, and of life and of my experience as a stranger in France. After dinner I came to town on my bike to drink coffee at La Buvette, but it was closed today, so I picked another cafe.

This other café is just down the street, and the coffee is cheap and strong. I cannot through words express the adoration I have been developing for Annecy. I feel as though it is a place where you can not only live, but live comfortably, it has about it a certain aura as if all is well in the world. Old streets, canals and buildings are filled with the sounds of French culture. These reflections are causing me to feel an internal disconnect from the culture of my upbringing. I want to be disconnected from the anger, hate, hostility, and superficial social importance's that I feel are so overrepresented by Southern Californian culture. All cultures suffer from some sort of negative impulses, but in my experiences here in Annecy, I feel as though they are less overwhelming.

I came here with the intention to live and to learn. In wanting to expand and learn more I find it so important to respect the local people and their culture. It is invigorating to watch them walk by in such a content and casual fashion, carrying on in their lives. I suppose I am envious that I must one day leave, and reclaim my own culture. I at times think this mode of life is becoming normal for me, that of being a stranger traveling in foreign lands and doing the best I can to adjust and assimilate. I suppose that anything can be beautiful if you are willing to open up to the idea of its beauty- perhaps even the things I had previously deemed to lack beauty.

Philosophy, friendship, and loving humanity are my primary objectives at the moment. I find myself daydreaming about not having to leave France, especially Annecy. Neither a picture nor a video could capture this ambiance that surrounds me, nor can my own linguistic creativity offer you a glimpse into the feeling of being here, and all that I have been seeing and experiencing. There are limitations on language and communicability. They are factors limiting my abilities of phenomenological description of my perceptions. There is something raw and powerful about the phenomena of experience itself, which cannot be thought about, described, or have its meaning thoroughly conveyed.

Of the characters whom most stand out, there is a man whom walks his dogs daily through the old town streets. His dogs are so large that they look more like small horses than dogs. I am noticing as well how much the French like to smoke- and I mean they really smoke a lot. These are but two small areas of focus that comprise the entire atmosphere, it would be impossible to describe everything, or even to notice the entirety of its peculiarities. For myself, at age 22 this is the perfect place to be swimming in my thoughts. I enjoy letting them loose their usual rigid structure, allowing them to flow more freely. I feel as though for once it is okay to be eccentric with my imagination.

Bobby is on his way. I think he is bringing a Russian friend with him. I am so fortunate to be experiencing such a mélange of cultures and of thought possibilities, swimming aimlessly about in so much newness.

Yet I must still wonder if there is a government in the world which is not in some way corrupt. Or is there a person whom is wholly conscious? I like to think we have this huge capacity for humanity and that human nature is generally good and mostly, I still think it is. However, in some instances of surface level reaction are the instances in which the greatest capacity is not actualized and is in fact skipped over by our hormonal programing- we react unconsciously and thusly the utility of our intellects fall by the way side.

In revision I actually think that human nature is indeterminately good or bad, I think that we through our experiences learn how to react to different stimuli. If we are well trained in virtue to know how and when to act in the ways which will produce good, then good will be the result of our actions. And likewise for bad and any mixture which may lay between the extremes of idealized 'good' and 'bad'. If our moral opportunities are subject to evolution as such, then we can at any point in our life if we so will it strongly enough change our operating systems, affecting our natures as human beings.

9 Juillet

The great musician Neil Young said, "Don't let it bring you down, its only castles burning, just find someone who is turning, and you will come around." The idea of moving on into the future is simply said, but so much more complicated to live through. It takes a lot of internal motivation to get over our past emotional conflicts, to eliminate our psychological borders and boundaries.

I need to be taken away in my mind. I have not been doing yoga nor meditating recently. I need to re-find my center for a few days here in the midst of my journey. Music is grounding, music soothes the soul, and even when we are the stranger "sometimes the songs that we hear are just songs of our own." –Grateful Dead

It is The Grateful Dead whom also sang, "Clowns to the left of me, jokers to the right. Here I am, stuck in the middle with you", the lyrics to this song make me think of how we are all lost in our own existential dilemmas, feeling as if we are surrounded by clowns and jokers, unable to recognize that our own existences are just as awkward as any others'. The song continues with, "trying to make some sense of it all, but I can see that it makes no sense at all", perhaps life does not exist to make sense, or to be communicable though we expect it to be. Yet it exists for and of itself, just to be. It is us the conscious beings who perceive existence and try to apply to it meaning and in doing so make some sense and much mess of the matter.

Listening to music can be a spiritual experience. Last night as I sat along Lac Annecy I watched the boats dance to no music. The boats clearly were unaware that they were dancing, yet I saw them dancing nonetheless. I contemplated whether or not they were singing songs to themselves or if they dance to no music just to dance. As if echoing Jerry Garcia of The Grateful Dead when he said, "Don't tread on me!" We cannot rightfully expect that boats need music to dance; just as they do not need water under them to be boats, only ideally to function as we have decided boats should function.

Stepping back, what a large and weighty responsibility we have to be responsible for creating our perception and defining our world. Meditation is so important for both Western and Eastern thinkers alike. To meditate is to connect with oneself and in doing so we decide how to best govern our energies. I find myself in discontentment with the degree to which my perception has been negative and negatively influenced by certain energies lately. If I think negatively then I am likely to react negatively towards things as well. Negativity can be a difficult obstacle to overcome. I believe that if I am conscious of this and know that it needs to change then ideally I should be able to begin to rethink these energy trends with the inclusion of new imaginative positive changes.

Expectations

What do expectations do? It seems as though when we assert our expectations we are claiming what we *predict* to be likely or possible. Yet when we place too great of a weight on our expectations we are setting ourselves up for being *discontent*. I think we should try to be open to experiences as they are, and not be too limited in how we expect them to play out. When we do not overexert our ideological expectations unto the actual world we are much more likely to find contentment with the state of things as they actually are and not as we had imagined them and wished for them to be. Things rarely play out just as we imagined, or just as we would have planned. We are only given access to such a small parcel of the whole universal truth, and we can only plan off of that which we *know*, and we can only imagine the things which our imagination can reach. We intrinsically have such limits.

As for these statements regarding expectations, I would like to make it clear that I am in no way asserting that one should have low, poor, or negative expectations. Rather, I am encouraging us to logically prepare our conscious to be able to disconnect from the emotional attachments that expectations foster; and to not allow the negative aftereffects of expectations not being met, or not being met under the exact means imagined. These types of virtue practices take lifetimes to work on, perfection will always be the expected goal, though we must know we will likely never reach that idealized perfection- this does not mean we should not want perfection. More simply put we should not let negativity seep into our consciousness and emotionally take imperfection too harshly upon ourselves just because we had expected perfection.

9 Juillet

Class today was great, I feel as if my French is improving every day.

I sometimes find that the best places to meditate are the places in which you are the most distracted. It takes even more work to isolate your consciousness and separate your mind from your body. This strange nuance to my meditation practices is similar to the idea that just as often, the hardest things to achieve are often the feats most worth pursuing.

To me bluntness and honesty seem less than a step away from each other. Sometimes what is meant to be honest seems blunt, and less the case that what is meant to be blunt, seems honest. Yet humans have two feet, and each 'free' individual whether they are conscious of their conscious choices or not, do chose where they place them. Eyes and mind, open or closed, fists clenched or hands extended to others we slowly step through the progression of our lives as perceived by our own subjective consciousness. We may strike a number of poses or hold many things; these particularities are different for each person and different at different times and in different places. We are all subject to the differences of the world. Regardless of the particular circumstances the mind is aware, and through its awareness has every capability of affecting the world.

Will

There have throughout time been numerous suggestions that human beings have freewill; just as many thinkers have worked to negate the existence of freewill and believe in a cosmic determinacy. Perhaps there is an ounce of validity to both of these two contrasting standpoints. When one really thinks hard about the possibility of freewill they quickly realize that it does not exist. This hard thinking on the subject of freewill should require a division of the terms as a primary approach to understanding the concept at large. We have a vast amount of will, but our freedom is non-existent because of circumstantial limitations that we face.

Firstly, I think that *will* itself must be explored. Do we not often sense a conflict within our will; a part of us wants a certain thing whilst some other fragment of our conscious seems to want another (this is not limited to a dichotomy, there may be a plurality of desires). If you *will* for this internal battle to be won by a particular desire, then your desire for that is strongest and through action it becomes your *apparent* will. This occurs even though there may have originally been a different option which some part of you wanted, a segment of your actual will. This means one must will to decide upon one's will before one's will can be enacted upon and bring choice and liberation into one's life experience.

It follows that in order for one to reevaluate and to create new solutions to solve new problems which arrive from new circumstances one must will to have the type of open mindedness which allows one to have a 'freedom' of will to decide upon imagining new solutions. That is to decide which will is going to be enacted into apparent will from all the possibilities of one's actual will. There can be many assumptions as to why one might will things in the first place. The most valid of which I will argue is for some type of gain. We will whatever will we think will work out best; 'what is best for us' can mean so many things in so many different situations- as it will also be different for different individuals. Yet wherever we calculate to find the greatest pragmatic utility we will send the will necessary to will one fragment of actual will to be greater than another so that we can will it into being; because we foresee that particular fragment of the full will spectrum as having the possibility of providing us with a greater benefit than anything else we could will, given the specifics of the situation.

This brings me back to my point which I assume many people will find opposition towards at first glance; entirely free-will does not exist. However, contextual will does exist and it provides us with a still astounding array of possibilities. If entirely freewill existed. I could transform into a dog, or a molecule, or teleport to anywhere I wish to be at the moment of my willing. These actions are not possible because of the impediment of factors external to my subjective consciousness's will. In those instances provided the particular factor is physics. The ways in which physics works makes all of these insertions of freewill into the actual world impossible. Physics however is a common, simple, and plainly apparent factor which limits the possibilities of our will. Other examples of factors include yet are not limited to: time, relationships, history, geographic occurrence, etc. All of these factors are circumstantial and are a function of a particular environment afflicting the desires of a particular individual's subjective consciousness.

So given the set of possibilities which exist within a given circumstance, a human's full spectrum of actual will may encompass all possibilities; so long as they can be weighed relative to the calculator. In recap the possibilities are defined by the factors in a circumstance, and what appears to be ones will is that fraction of will which they devote the most will towards. So we still have an astounding amount of will, but it is always in a realistic sense, and not in an entirely free sense that we could immediately will anything which we may think of into actual states of being.

This means that we are then slaves to our environment. Our will is entirely ours, but its capacities of enactment are defined by our environment. When we are calculating things and intentionally will which wills we will most to will that we will notice our wills coming to us as we will them. This desire and will cycle works most efficiently when we are correctly interpreting our possibilities and willing our favorites. Those wills which give us the greatest benefit towards our being, are the most pragmatic wills. I do not know that I have ever met anyone who flawlessly and most pragmatically wills without failure by way of miscalculation, but as we see the results of our wills coming to us the motivation to assert our will in such a consciously reflective manner increases. In a sense it is as if willing is a game which we never completely can win, but we can always play a little bit better every time.

You could as well suppose that even if you are not aware that you are playing this 'game', you are still playing it. But as you are unconscious of it, it is unlikely that you are playing very well. As one raises consciousness and draws from their memories of the past and applies that knowledge into new occurrences in new circumstances, they develop the abilities to fuse their imagination into their memories to make the most of newness; in effect creating a fusion of traditional knowledge and imagination. This understanding of conscious play within ones' wills, and ones' habituations towards preferences, or favorites as I have called them, allows for our freedom as much it allows for our manipulation. As it is obvious that there are so many more whom do not engage in such *intellectual conscious play* with their will than there are people whom are aware that they are playing the game.

This gives time for conscious players to construct labyrinths that render lesser aware-conscious players to encounter great difficulty in achieving their desires and foster an environment in which they are forced to struggle without much efficiency. For example: someone once willed there to be a currency; he stood a pragmatic gain of simplifying trade interactions. Later currency became a standard factor in trade circumstances. As we in modern times are bombarded with advertising and social trends of mass consumerism, we find our environment has changed from a currency of trade for necessity of survivorship, into an environment of constant trade and monetary importance as a result of the prevalence for economic advantage being highly pragmatically calculated and highly socially desirable. These tactics render many players to be so confused that they never really stand a chance at competing in the game.

In many cases buyers actually think that they will to buy products, when in reality many of those products are the very same products whose advertisements have been so frequently engrained into their memories that they by association of past inference will reselect them time and time again. This occurs in some instances even though they may know there is an alternative which is actually of higher quality or in some way more beneficial. It is because unconscious players will is so much weaker than a conscious players, that they will repetitively miscalculate for example the pragmatic utility of name brand recognition with actual quality of product.

We do what is familiar and generally tend to avoid newness as it places us 'outside of our comfort zones'. Yet those things which are now familiar were once new and replaced other things that were familiar. This cycle of familiarity and rediscovery is what makes humanity compelling and interesting. We see that innovation is our blessing; it gives us the inspiration to create a world around us that we willed into being. One may say that they dislike the city or town that they live in, and they will to be in a particular other location. It is possible for them to travel and move to that location, if it really is that they so will to place themselves there more so than they will the things which will stand in the way of that becoming the apparent will, and not just a fraction of actual will.

Those 'other things' however get in the way of one packing up their bags and leaving. We realize we will miss our family, friends, familiar places where our cherished memories occurred, etc. These other parts of the actual will stem from deeply emotional linked familiarity, and if they are more willed upon than the will to no longer live in that city over the preferred city, then the apparent *will* will be that they wish to stay there- even if the actual will also contains in part the will to live somewhere else. It is our innovation which gives us the ability to step in and out, around and through our ideas to look at them from a multitude of dimensions- rather than just that same old familiar perspective in which we refuse to accept change. As for the classic false 'in the box' 'out of the box' dichotomy, I offer a third solution. Be the box. Define the parameters- determine for yourself what is inside and outside of the box. You imagined the box in the first place. Relate to and connect with both modes simultaneously rather than segregating the self into a miniscule category. I am the box. Be the box.

9 Juillet

After dinner I find myself back at the café with Bobby. We have so much fun sitting here in the old medieval cobblestone streets of Annecy, at our favorite café. At which we meet locals and world travelers alike, everyone with a different face, background, story, personality, etc. It is a good place to think, and it is enthralling to think in such thoughtful company. I drink wine, yet more often I order café noir après café noir, après encore plus (black coffee after black coffee, after more and more). At times the French would joke with me about my late night coffee drinking habits. To which my wise friend Bobby the Dutchman replied, "It doesn't matter what you drink, as long as you enjoy it." I agreed. There are so many different types of people with so many different types of drink. Each orders that which pleases them, as it pleases them to be in public, and to drink with their comrades.

I am at times embarrassed to be American here. Especially with the tension between Edward Snowden and the NSA, there is a growing anti-American sentiment, and I feel it often. Even though I am myself, just another human being, and there is nothing to be ashamed about. I think. It does however make me ponder, what is temperance? How can we even possibly find correct action in this sea of change? There is too much is constantly flowing and changing all around us. As soon as we think that we have some idea or concept of what is going on we awaken to a new and different reality. Even in the last twenty minutes since I last wrote something, the rain and summer thunderstorm blew in. And water began rushing down the ancient streets of Annecy, la Vielle Ville. C'est vraiment un orage du change.

Our drinks disappear, people walk by, and I would even dare say that the French girls sitting at the table next to us are looking more appealing with each passing minute. All these minute particular aspects that are available to the human subjective conscious stream are constantly changing. It is the same café, yet the atmosphere, l'air, is constantly different. 'Why?' Is the question that Heraclitus did not apparently ask; why must things change?

I suppose that life, and all of our perception of its progression would be fundamentally impossible without the existence of change. It is so necessary for our existence. Before motion started, before 'time began' as some might put it, before energy and matter collided, there was everything and there was nothing. As in accordance with the wise words of Lao Zu, there was only the Tao, and from the Tao all opportunity- all possibilities flow. They disappear, and they return, only to be thrown back in and out of existence. And all of this occurs in moments unperceivable by the human subjective consciousness; mainly because it occurs outside the scope of our perceptual abilities.

<u>Part Five</u>

QU'EST-CE QUE
C'EST NORMAL?

10 Juillet

Life becomes both weirder and more interesting day by day, the more I open myself up to the newness the more I have on my plate of experience. Last night Bobby, some of my friends from school and I saw an amazing show. A stage was erected in Annecy where the heart of the city meets the lake. The spectacle was a fire-drumming performance for the public on account of la fête nationale. The entertainment consisted of a drum line group, and fireworks accompanied by lots of other pyrotechnics. I marveled at just how many people from Annecy and all the surrounding areas turned out to watch the show. Someone in the rear of the crowd handed out long sparkler sticks that were passed forwards through the audience towards the stage. The smiling faces passed torch after torch through the crowds. There was such a friendly sense of community, I felt as though everyone in attendance were fellow humans passing torches, celebrating life and liberty together. Afterwards, we went to the café… and somehow we ended up at Rivers, a 'club' popular to tourists and a venue which I do not care for.

Do we not reject at times other's conceptions of reality? We call them wrong and untrue from our limited spheres of knowledge. Are we so desperate in asserting our own 'Will to Power' that we sacrifice our humanity, and disparage others whom differ from us because of contextual circumstances outside either of our control? I would certainly hope that if this is so, we can change it! We can at least to be mindful of these occurrences and our power of play within them.

What a strange and uncomfortable position it can be to try and fit one's mind into the confines of another's. What beautiful but few modes we have of conveyance from one mind to another. Perhaps this is the other side of the coin of our great intellectual capacities. We make our own worlds so immense, complex, and individualized that we cannot always find a way to merge our consciousness with others. The merging of consciousnesses creates some form of <u>plural existential understanding</u>. We can all have our own relative existential understanding, and these understandings do not need to make sense to others.

I can never be too sure of my belief or disbelief in fate or consider myself a subscriber to the notion that 'all things happen for a reason'. I do like to think that all things have a cause and a corresponding causation. I think that all things which happen do in fact happen. As for the reason- we apply the reason as an after-thought. It comes about through analysis and organization of the phenomena into our memories as they fall and fit into our schema of understanding the world.

If it were possible to rearrange the psychic reflexes to make room for the appreciation of other entities per-ceptual modes we would fare better as a species and as the guardian inhabitants of such a wonderful part of the universe.

I feel the need to bring my current environment up. It is consuming me, it is effecting me, and undoubtedly as well I am affecting it. Immediately before I started writing this current segment I parked my bike in the garden of the house I am staying at on Rue de Joeseph Duchine in Annecy, France. The garden is beauti-ful and bustling with life! There is food growing and throughout the garden you find an array of beautiful flowers. This garden is also the perfect place to acciden-tally step on a dying bee.

As if to prevent him from dying in vein, he made good use of his adornment. His stinger, as it plunged into my foot moments before the time of his actual death- the end of his current form of existence. I pulled out the stinger and sat back down to unwind in my reflections.

My unwinding was interrupted by my host mother stepping out onto the balcony above and summoning me for dinner. I rushed upstairs so as not to be disrespectful to such an amazing cook! I am always very satisfied after eating her meals. Following dinner I plan to go to the café as usual

14 Juillet

After a long day of school, picnicking at the lake with the Russian girls, an American named Ben, and of course Bobby, it is nice to be at the café. The streets are crowded and full of performers, art and live music. The Southern French Alps during the summer are quite the place to be. As the snow clears in the mountains everyone is eager to be out and about for any reason, whenever possible. Tonight they have a great reason. It is the fête national and a Friday night as well! Tomorrow I depart for Geneva; it should be quite an adventure. This will be my first time in Switzerland

How quickly life and experience can come and go. You never know when you are going to lose opportunities that you think are not going to disappear on you. Even if you sit still and calm your mind to try and capture them, the world will keep moving and changing around you. The present moment is always evanescent.

Speaking of the changing of the environment, I received some good news today. My good friend and fellow philosopher from Hawaii named Mathew Kalahiki is on his way to France at last, he is the last of our group to arrive. I cannot even express exactly how excited I am to have another academic philosopher here, espe-cially a Hawaiian one. I think that as a result of his arrival, Annecy and the whole experience here is about to change for the better. Yet still, I am grateful that I have met so many people from so many countries.

Separation and Isolation

Despite our aspirations for being connected with the greater entirety of reality, humans are subject to an existential condition which renders them, as we have recently discussed, trapped their own conscious separate from all other minds. This means that we will always feel separated from others, and that we will always feel somewhat isolated. Even when preforming acts together we will always be in some way removed by the unique perspectives that only our own personhoods' could ascertain. What accompanies this sensation of isolation is pain. This pain comes from the feelings of incongruence with existence

On a more personal reflection upon this topic I think that we may find at times that those other beings which we thought we knew so well, and which we considered to understand surprise us. Their underlying personality aspects sometimes lay dormant and reveal themselves as they pass in and out of activation. Sometimes these surprises will delight us, at other times they will cause us to want to separate from that individual. Just as easily as we may build them we can deconstruct the barriers which separate us. We can remove feelings and sensations of isolation as we attempt to reconnect to a more harmonious state of being. I hope that these occurrences are aspects of cycles, and that we can take comfort in believing that they will arrive and that they will pass. We may feel connected at one moment, and separated at another, but each will pass and the cycle will once again come full around.

A Shitty Lunch

15 Juillet

What a day! I took a bus along with my schoolmates to Geneva. We took a tour around the city with the group. Mathew and I had the chance to talk a lot. Mathew and I hung out with two of my Russian friends Anna and Liliia. We ate pizza together on a terrace in Geneva. Liliia was all dressed up, and I jokingly believe she was hoping to find a rich husband while in the city that day; at least she was dressed as if she was. Classy and very euro-sophisticated. While we were sitting on the terrace eating something strange happened to Liliia's head. At first she just held her hand over her head, and looked disgruntled. Mathew and I turned away from our conversation and asked her what her expression was for. She at first decidedly did not want to tell us what had happened. Then she turned and stated, 'fine, I will tell you what has happened" in her heavy east Russian accent. "A bird poo-ded on me"! To which we could simply not hold our laughter. We felt bad, so I asked the waitress where my friend could find the restroom. Whilst Liliia and Anna were inside cleaning the bird poop out of her hair, Mathew and I continued eating our pizza. A few moments had passed when a bird pooped on my shirt as well. When Lilia returned from the restroom feeling much better, we informed her that a bird had pooped on me as well. She had thought we were kidding until I showed her the mark on my shirt from which I had whipped away the poop and she finally shed a smile.

I assume that most can resonate with the horror of a bird having pooped on them. We are able to use our imagination to understand how uncomfortable it is when a bird poops on us. It is commonly most humorous when things occur to other people. Someone falls and we laugh, yet when it is us who falls we do not always instinctually laugh at our own slippages. But why not laugh when it happens to ourselves and take the whole ordeal light heartedly? When we read any phenomena negatively rather than positively, we open up the doors for negativity to enter into our perceptions, our experience, and into our existences! Instead during these very human experiences I think it best to implore one's sense of humor.

Could it be that some people can never experience the joy of light heartedness? Could it be that one's magnetisms and thought frequencies can be so negatively connoted that they will never explore the joy of positivity? I think I would live a more pleasant existence if I found joy more often than not- even when a bird poops on me.

17 Juillet

I am beginning to get used to my new routine here. Today I went to class, as I do every day. Afterwards

I went to the park next to the lake for a picnic with friends. Following the picnic Mathew and I went to the beach. Whilst surrounded by so much newness, the existential malaise creeps in upon me, from within my own mind, encompassing my being. Yet despite these periods of malaise something inside of me is driving me towards my new experiences. I have been exploring my intrigue in being lost. No matter where you are, at home or in a foreign country humans are always lost and always confused- trying to find their way in an ever-changing reality.

As I cruise through the streets of old Annecy I am delighted by all of the beautiful flowers which line all the canals and balconies. Centuries old buildings still function and stand in all their different design and colors. I must be about as lost as a human could be- swimming in a sea of confusion.

Right now I feel nauseous because this old French lady wearing entirely too much perfume sat down next to me, I feel the need to smoke a cigarette. Not only to mask the awful smell but as a well to mask the awkwardness of her slowly pulling her skirt up her leg. She caught me looking out of the corner of my eye, out of my naïve curiosity, and it is only encouraging her further- My mistake. I think all egos like to pretend that they are flawless, that they have some kind of authority that others do not, but really, we all have flaws and they stem from our unrealistic expectations of perfection.

Names...

Names, what are they?- Ways of an individual asserting that she knows something about the state of things in the world. What a remarkable claim we state when we declare that we know the name of a thing. We undergo a complex process as thinking humans in which we name things, their characteristics, aspects, and functions as a methodology of asserting our conscious dominance over things. If these things can be named, and described thoroughly, then we feel powerful as if our minds are so great that these miniscule things can be thought around. Real objects once given a name can be removed from their actual being and moved elsewhere or even done away with within the confines of our ideological thought space. This act of naming and using names gives humans a linguistic sense of supreme dominance over their surroundings. Furthermore for human life to function in the ways which culture and society have evolved thus far this process of naming things for ideological domination is completely necessary.

I am curious as to what are the limits of asserting intellectual powers such as the 'naming of things and stuff'? Clearly culture, language, and availability of occurrences which could be named and examined will have an effect on the overall hermeneutic intent of a words usage and contextual positioning inside of rhetorical compositions. Is it a wrongful abuse of intellectual power to rob another culture of their words, and assert our own manipulations of being (language) upon them so that they must work within a context rigged for them to be exploited? Or is this a natural stage in cognitive evolution?

It is because the nature of emotional scaring runs so

deep that the trauma hurt the souls of those traumatized, any conscious and or virtuous being would wish to inflict upon others the lowest amount of emotional scaring possible. If we use community and human connection to love and to heal each other, bringing in with open arms positivity, we are using our capacities efficiently. However, when we abuse these intellectual powers and assert negativity through exploitation, control and traumatic scaring of others, then I ask; what are we stating we believe humanity to be?

It appears to be that many of our greatest weaknesses are also great strengths, only they are treated thusly in a negative sense, and the reflections of this expressed negativity stain our own consciousness's. We scar not only others but as well we scar ourselves when we exert hatred towards others.

Arguably, if one is *'vibe-sensitive'* then these energies exchanged in human interactions should be incredibly self-revealing. Complicated; What a good word, making good use of English, to describe the overwhelming scope of the human condition- as unimaginably unique, intricate, and complicated. But there is always hope in the heart that wills it, there is always an experience to be gathered, and there is always love to spread, if we can just figure out how to get through all the mess and confusion. Together, we can overcome these difficulties that our own names superimpose upon us from the moment we receive them, from the moment we are enslaved to those whom know our names.

Identity

Although in our youth we are named, we define who and what our identity is to be throughout the course of our lives. The ways we perceive, the thoughts we have, the thoughts about our thoughts, our actions, and our reflections on all previously mentioned aspects form over time our identities. While some may know us by name, or know some aspects about us, the true artisan the true master craftsman behind our personhoods is always the self. An intensely intimate and delicate creation the identity is. We guard it at times, whilst at others we may reveal too much of it. We have it when we go to sleep every night, it follows us even in our dreams, and when we wake up it is there to carry with us throughout the longevity of our days. We must learn to love it, and to make our identity and our place in the world by way of it, one of positivity, and one which promotes the type of environment in which goodness will flourish. This is crucial to a conception of a road to happiness.

Fear and 'Strangers'

Over time humanity has accumulated wounds- physical, emotional, and spiritual. These wounds block our connectedness and block the flow of energy through each individual, society and humanity at large. Often times when pushed out of normality, or out of one's comfort zone the result is a rejection of the new experience. This rejection is the root of the blockage, and the root of the socially programed rejection is fear. Fear of difference and fear of change then are what limits us most. They flow through this river of action and reaction, and where they dam up the current the result is suffering.

It is not that this fear and the rejection complex have not served humans well at certain times, for certain persons, under certain circumstances of human evolution. However, I do feel at times that this attitude of fear has become far too habitual and far too socially engrained. I witnessed it first-hand growing up in crowded Southern California, and have seen traces of it everywhere I have ever traveled. It pushes away person from person, separated by an imaginary wall of difference, ripping apart what could be beautiful seams of humanity. If subjective consciousness's pay attention to when they are falling privy to fear, and when the fear is fundamentally necessary for survival and or general welfare we can find balance and remediation from this run-away fear complex.

This topic reminds me of my time spent in Lyon. I was far out of my comfort zone as I passed the night at the train station. I met strangers, some of which I chose not to trust. I did not trust them not because I am systematically untrusting, but because I exercised discernment and only chose to trust the individual whom I chose to trust. Choice here is the key to balancing these fears. Humans in most instances have the liberty to choose, and because of this liberty you have the option to choose not fear, and to reprogram yourself in a way more conductive of your spiritual being, playing with your human emotions, and alleviating your physical suffering. Idealism may seem at times farfetched but the principles that can be drawn from it are what change people's lives. If you are not scared to change your life, you will make the decisions that your liberty allows for and thusly you improve your being through it, and drive yourself away from the pain and scaring that fear and suffering place upon humanity.

I would encourage anyone to engage strangers, to find how friendly people can be. That is to avoid ideologies full of harsh judgment, and to find ways to accept and appreciate the differences in each and every person. A world without individual flavors would be boring, and our pallets are boring until we paint them with the colors of the world, and all the stimuli of the back alleys, promenades, and vast countrysidess of humanity.

We may place the blame on the world, because we are afraid of the world and our fears limit us from enacting as our deepest desires may influence us towards. However, after the fact of the world, the cognitive subjective conscious always has the ability to choose its form of encoding. It can take even a fearful encounter, and reshape it by perspective shift into that of love, growth, and unity. As the band 311 stated in their song *Speak Easy*, "it is so liberating to be free". Neither freedom nor liberty exists as facts or naturally occurring states of affairs in the world, we must consciously and willfully assert their existences. I think that they only exist as ideas, ideas are prisons for concepts, and they are always asserted by consciousness. We may think that they come from an external source, yet as these thoughts are internal, we should pay mind to the fact that they are our internal ideologies. Who is in charge here anyway? The thoughts which occur to us as reactions or ourselves as active agents and liberated beings with choice?

The many strangers I have met, the many times I took it upon my liberty to be open to new experiences have provided me with blessings. Blessings come in the form of memories, wonderful friends, and a happy- life validating sense of human harmony. It does not matter what context any person is coming from, we all have the ability to find communion and unity with each other. There are so many more similarities than there are differences, but often we are too ignorant and fearful to be open to accepting these relationships into our perceptual realities. Confusion is good.

17 Juillet

This reoccurrence is haunting- that I no longer know what I am thinking, nor do I know how to write, but something and only one thing seems obvious, my own nausea. The awkwardness of living can at times seem overwhelming. Once I get on my bike and go home, it will all be normal once again, and my nausea will fade as my comfort returns. Maybe all I needed was something familiar, some reggae music to make me feel at home- even now when I am far away from any place that I can truly call home. It seems as though even though I enjoy writing in my little red book, though I notice that at times it blocks my humanity during social occasions. My Russian friend Anna, whom ate with us in Geneva, yet was not pooped on… made a joke about how frequently I read and write in public places, particularly at La Buvette.

"Dear Diary,
Today, she looked at me with a beautiful smile."

She suggested that this is how my diary must read. She is very kind, and in cases like this, she shows her spectacular sense of humor! As well I think it is quite awkward to write with someone looking over my shoulder, they act as if they are not paying attention, but you know more than anything they want to know what you are reading or writing, especially when they keep making jokes in Russian to each other, laughing, and looking back at me.

Little do they know I am writing about what they are saying! I might be in my own world when I write, but I am more connected than people may assume; even at times like this… To appease my friend Anna I let her look at my other books of philosophy. There are many moments in which I just like to think and write and laugh at myself and my own thoughts. I think that it is good to have good humor towards my own existence. Since things so frequently change, you cannot take anything too seriously. It is probably bad for your health to do so anyways.

To get angry, to be negative adds nothing positive to the world, only more negativity. We must face our human flaws rooted in emotion, and instead incite in ourselves good emotions, even in the midst of negative situations. The French have a beautiful way of doing just this, by using the expression, "c'est la vie". Life is going to be as it is, and there is no use getting all worked up about it.

19 Juillet

What an interesting day I had yesterday, always a new adventure! I left school with Moses and Mathew; we went to the Supermarché and bought baguettes and sausages for lunch. We ate in the cemetery. I think it is good to occasionally eat with the dead and keep them company. Afterwards I went home to change into an aloha shirt and meet with Liliia and Anna at their house, they cooked dinner for Marcel, Bobby and I. We ate, drank wine, and played a game. The game where you write a well-known person's name on a card and pass it to the person next to you, they then place the card on their forehead and the group takes turns asking questions in trying to figure out whose name is posted on their forehead.

After dinner, the game, and dessert, Bobby and I departed together and road our bikes to La Buvette du Marché- as usual. We ran into our French friend Lucia, she was drinking there with her friends for her birthday. The café was quite packed this night, and was a real party! I had the pleasure of meeting Lucia's friend named Sarah. Sarah and I sat down at a table outside and talked film and philosophy, then smoked a cigarette on the street before going to La Telephone Rouge, the best night club in Annecy. I drank rum and coke and danced to deep house until 3 am, at which point I returned home. I am not sure if I have mentioned it enough but I really enjoy dancing, especially to good music in a venue with a good ambiance.

Sitting in our favorite café is always a pleasurable experience. The service could not be more excellent! I really like the French attitude towards work! The coffee is very good and the intersection of Rue St. Claire and Rue de la Gare is always busy and full of interesting blends of people. This evening when Bobbly farted he said, "if you smell something... it is not a fire" He can be so Dutch at times, yet I find his sense of liberty and enjoyment of life amusing and always enjoy his company.

Birds, the survivors of a set of genes that began long before humans inhabited the planet, jumping and flying about with keen senses looking for what they need; food, water, sex. Are not all animals similar in needs? Do we not all enjoy wanting what we want amidst pursuing that which we need? I think that we do! I hope that we do! I hold onto hope, I cling to my notion and ideas as not only are they the only thing I want, but coincidentally are the only thing which can never be stolen from me.

I live not for the possession of objects, but for the experience; I live for living, and for living do I live-through tough days and wonderful moments alike. I have no choice but to continue onwards with my hope and my ideas. I keep thinking that life is very funny and bleakly bizarre. I do not know if you noticed but I have been living it all this time, and most of the time I am laughing. Sharing of laughter and experience is certainly one of the best parts of being human. Anything which makes me laugh, I seek out for enjoyment!

Bobby and I are planning a trip to camp out on top of Semnoz. We are going to set up his tent which he brought with him to France from Amsterdam alongside the road. Tomorrow the Tour de France is coming through our little town- Annecy. I am overwhelmingly excited to witness this event in person. I am expecting the whole ordeal to be a grand adventure in itself. I am also expecting, as usual, to have my mind blown!

Newness

What is newness? It appears to be a momentary revelation. Whatever is now is new. Even a mountain or a stream seen many times before is new upon every sighting. Even seemingly still objects like a mountain are changing and shifting every single moment- despite the fact that lingering in the mind are memories of a past vision of the mountain. That past vision is no longer new- it is a memory is of the past. If the eyes are closed even for a moment- as with blinking, upon the reopening you are faced again with a nuanced mountain. More frequently we will be conscious of experiences of newness which regards things which are new in that they were previously unfamiliar to us- inconnu, the newest of all nuances.

When faced with a familiarity, we have little fear; the potential newness of the experience is only slightly differentiated from what we are by the past prepared to experience. We may sense a slight anxiety to see a deficit in our expectations playing out in actuality, yet because of our familiarity the fear invoked from these stimuli is minimal. The greater fears come from that with which we are unfamiliar. These new nuances evade our memories, we have no idea precisely where we can place our expectations, and frequently this leads humans to be programed to fear the newness. What if instead of fearing newness, we embraced it? What if everything new was another flavor, another color never seen before? - Something which holds a capacity for great beauty. Whether familiar or unfamiliar in nature, each nuance has the potentiality for being beautiful, and for enhancing the spread of universal positivity.

Part Six

LE TOUR D'ANNECY

20 Juillet

Bobby and I purchased tickets for été, *a bus which only runs during the summer. It takes persons, their bikes, and their gear from the town of Annecy up to the top of Mt. Semnoz. We took off just before sunset. By the time our bus reached the top of the mountain it was raining heavily, and there was a thunderstorm. We had taken with us Bobby's tent, but also our two bikes which we bought at a thrift store called La Bizarre in Annecy. Our bikes were cheap, yet they are our only reliable mode of transportation with which to travel to and from our studies. We arrived at the finish line atop the mountain, and got off with our gear and bikes. We waved goodbye to our friendly bus driver, and started riding a ways back down the course. In the thunderstorm with heavy bags of gear and insufficient stopping power from the old weak breaks we decided to pull over onto a campground we had seen from the bus. People were sitting in cars, sleeping in tents, and RV's lined up all along the road. It was pouring rain, and lightning strikes were occurring all over and around the mountain. We moved aside the railings and ran our bikes towards a large white tent.*

We heard music and cheerful (dry) people shouting from within the tent, as we came near it Bobby said. "Do you hear that? It is Dutch music, they are Dutch!" And we ran up the hill towards the tent and threw our bikes down and it seems as though we sort of fell into the tent, soaking wet with our gear. We heard them as we had approached the opening muttering something which sounded like hello, yet was indecipherable, and we could not place the language. They were some twelve Dutchmen of all sizes and statures drinking and singing inside of a French café tent. The tent was operated by a commune of French hippies fundraising off of the cycling event. They had beer, snacks, crepes, coffee, and French style lunches with cheese and bread. The French hippies were excited that finally someone in the tent spoke French. The Dutchmen were all very kind and in great spirits for the event, yet in their celebrations they were rowdy. Their rowdiness was making the French patron nervous. He asked me in French to please ask them to let go of the bars that hold up the tent, I relayed that message then to Bobby in English, and he telephoned it back to them in Dutch. They respectfully obliged.

The French hippies and I were now officially friends. Bobby and I drank lots of beer, danced and sang all night, oh and we ate a whole tub of candy! The stars that night were amazing, it had cleared up a bit before we headed out to Bobby's tent which we had set up inside of the large white tent, once it was erected we carefully placed outside along the road. Despite the fact that my French had greatly improved over the previous few weeks, I still had had trouble convincing the French hippies to allow me to set up a tent, inside of their tent.

We had packed a lot of food to take up with us, and as we smoked and drank strong rum in the tent long after the Dutchmen had all gone to sleep. I began to ponder…. What is food but the things we eat? Just then Bobby's iPod died, and he shouted that "iPods are not to be trusted" in his funny Dutch accent. I am really glad to have such a good friend here. I continued the music using the empty tub of candy as a drum. After playing for a while I heard voices outside. I stopped playing and walked outside to meet them. It was a small group of Jr. High School aged French school children whom were walking up and down the roads wanting to meet the people who had come to camp out on their mountain for the event. There were all funny, and we spoke French together until they found out I was American, at which point they wanted to practice their English.

Bobby and I fell asleep after singing and listening to another group of campers' music as it carried across the campsite. We had a tent but I have no sleeping bag. I decided to make a bed with towels and used my back pack as a pillow. When I awoke everything was a blur, I was terribly hung over, and brain processes were at a near standstill. I sat at the door of the tent to smoke a cigarette. The air was filled with the sound of bells, so much so that I became bewildered. Cars, RVs, and people lined the road; many more than were there the previous night when we had arrived. From the little port hole of the tent all that I could see that was moving was a van. My brain was so incredibly groggy and since I had not yet had my coffee, I was curious as to the overwhelming sound of bells and its source yet utterly unable to actually think about anything. All I had to work with in motion were the people filled in along the barricades on the road side for the race and a van which was pulling into the campground through the barricades. Logically I thought the van was full of bells. When the van moved far enough through the gate that what lay behind it was now visible, I saw across the road a lush green hillside, covered in hundreds of hopping goats with bells attached to their necks.

The café which we camped outside was called Buvette Du Alpes, which was run by the awesome French hippies of whom I previously discussed. They live up here permanently and Bobby and I were fortunate enough to see their camp today. They camp in large Yurt huts with clear ceilings so they can see the stars in the summer, and they build and live in igloos during the cold winters. One of my favorite moments I shared with these hippies was when I walked into their tent the morning of Tour de France. It was buzzing with persons from many different countries who had come out to witness the event. Julian who was in charge of the café sighted me and shouted in English, "My friend!!!" and all of the workers cheered, it was both very surprising and beautiful. I then got a cup of coffee, and a crêpe, my day was ready to begin.

I felt as though I was really embracing the newness of my circumstances. In doing so I made new friends, shared Europe's love for cycling and cycling culture, and got to see a warm welcomed glimpse into the lives of these kind mountain-dwelling folk. There seems to be something about the country, when things slow down that makes people seem more like people than they do in the city. It is something I enjoy, and something which makes me dread going back into the large cities where people not only push and shove others around frequently- worse they do not care that they do so, and regard it as necessities of survivorship when they feel compelled to do so.

Newness was working for me atop Semnoz; I was alive and tingling with wonder. It is moments such as this when you are pushed forwards by your excitement. The motivation of new and newer newness creeps upon you and makes you want to know what is around the next bend. It pulls you in towards it, caught in its gravitational pull. Those kinds of motivations towards newness can be what brings you into the possibility of being a better individual mentally, emotionally, physically, and spiritually. When I conquered the possibility of having fears, and embraced the newness, I had embraced the beauty of life.

An Abstract Vision

There is an apparent connection between the subconscious mind and the confines of actuality. Our entire life is confined by our unique subjective streams. What flows into our minds belongs to the world, and what flows through our minds are our thoughts about those things. These two modes of stream represent what we get out of life- that is what we gather from that which surrounds us; as well as what we put into life, mainly we add ideas. Our ideas are by their very nature intended to differ from the ideas of others. They exist not in that which flows into our mind, but our attempts to grab onto fragments of what is flowing through our own stream. All the while during this feat we are trying to accumulate these idea particles from other streams. We are subject to both the flow of the world surrounding us, and our own conscious stream. It requires much determination and diligence to isolate that which flows into our minds from that which flows around us; even more-so for us humans to isolate that which flows through any other persons mind.

Our minds have developed intimately throughout our lives off of social platforms that developed over the course of thousands of years of human history and evolution prior to even our first thought. Have you ever taken a moment to try to count all of the thoughts you have had in your life? I have, it seems as though at any point in one's life this is impossible to calculate. Our brains shed off subconsciously the aspects of the flowing world that are not 'needed' for conscious attention. Those sections brought from the flow in through the minds conscious stream are those deemed most important for survival and those necessary for undergoing other desired superfluous human activities.

There are so many social aspects of humanity which are not necessary for our survival as living beings on a life bearing planet, yet our minds seem to crave them and choose to fixate upon the continuum of actions and reactions. We become hyper concerned then about the inaccessible conscious streams of other individuals, hoping that their praise will determine our feelings of validation and self-adequacy. This infatuation with information which does not belong to us causes us distress and malaise. Ideologically both religion and neo-consciousness movements such as 'being' and 'now' consciousness have been provided to attempt to help us fix these issues of human confusion.

The past and the future can seem just as important as now, and especially when it comes to sacrificing the future for something available now, we should think, think, and rethink a notion. We so unfortunately are not able to freeze the streams at a moment of bliss and prolong it into the future, or to pull it backwards blinding ourselves from the past by its banner. Eventually human needs will creep into our thoughts, and a desire for social interaction impedes upon the still momentary mind. Perhaps we will eventually find that stillness in death- the death as well of our egos. Concurrently we should utilize the momentum of living whilst it is most fully available to us; live whilst alive.

The confusion we face inside of our own conscious streams can be terrifying, unless we are able to efficiently change our perspective towards it. The difficulty in changing perspective is that it requires immense movement. More particularly that movement must breech an escape velocity from the preexisting mentality. Theoretically this would mean breaking free from the positional confines of the origin of agitation and moving into a new location which offers the desired tranquil or pleasure-full disposition. Energy is the main component required to accelerate momentum into a perspective shift. You may ask yourself where this energy comes from; I would refer you to our most innate human drives of hunger, sleep, shelter, and sex. From these drives and combinations there-of we draw energy into our physical being and channel it into the kinds of motion that we find to be necessary to complete our desires and to will our wills; this occurs no matter how intricate or how simple our desires may be. Effectively, the more balanced we are the better our energy.

At base without these drives, without this need and reward sequencing we would not have our physical existence ensured, causing us to forfeit our internal conscious thought streams, and as well the prospect of having our prized and beloved social desires fulfilled, and you can forget about procreation altogether. We must recognize the basis of human operational platforms before we may hope to have much efficiency in channeling our subjective conscious streams into creating efficacy in the world of actuality. In the process we create the world that we wish in our dreams as it becomes future realities due to our cognitive assertions.

Furthermore on this topic, since none of our subjective streams will ever be an accurate capturing of the reality flowing around us, we should not get ruffled by the mismatching's of our own perceptions with the perceptions of others. Interactions and sharing in social atmospheres are all invoked by our programming that we have been exposed to over the course of our lives, the same which tells us that we need to achieve a certain degree of social importance to find our own internal fulfillment. The truth is most people will never reach these idealized levels of social importance.

It is not their goal, aspiration, and none of the vibes which they emit operate at a frequency conductive of making this aspiration manifest. If this is your wish, wish it for yourself. Wasting time, effort and most importantly energy upon trying to force someone else to think your thoughts, wish your wishes, and dream your dreams is ridiculous. It either happens because tonal frequencies of desire, need, and actuality match- or it does not occur because there is a mismatch. But the existence of both matches and miss matches are completely natural and supplement the dynamic beauty of life through the potentialities of coexistence.

For example you could have one gentleman who believes that jazz is the greatest genre of music ever created, and he chooses to dedicate his whole life to becoming a great stand-up bass player- and one whom only plays jazz baselines. At the same time you may have another fellow who thinks the most divine sound is that of a harp, and he plays a magically enchanting harp. Neither is the first man wrong for his love of jazz and of the stand-up bass, nor is the second man wrong in any actual capacity for his love the harp and musical lore.

It may be that if you put the two musicians in the same room and asked them to play together that their styles tonal frequencies (simplified and understood as sound) might clash in a god-awful conglomeration of two incompatible styles of music. However, suppose that the two were able to get out of the intimacy of their own frequency comfort zones, and find a way to respect each other's autonomy and work together, they could possibly make a new genre of music, or combined they might produce the most beautiful pattern of sound ever woven. Thirdly they might be best playing their own style to separate audiences never to be fused together, etc. Moreover, the decision towards praise or disgust residing in the audience is a relative function of that person's historical experience of music, tonal frequency, and expectations of what music or either instrument/ genre 'should' sound like all filtered through their own unique preferences.

Futility of Self-Separation and the Ego

Expectations, we all have them. They are an aspect of our willing upon the world. We all wish and have will power, a power which we ourselves create in our minds, and utilize by externalizing the power to affect the world around us. There is a limited prospect for the internal stream of consciousness to affect the vastness of the stream surrounding, flowing through and into our individual conscious streams. In order to have much efficiency at all, the ego develops itself. It is an assertive and wanting aspect of human consciousness. It wills to will itself upon everything that it wills. Concordantly if a hyperinflation of the ego is undergone there is a separation from actuality, into a spectrum of reality that is symbolic of a self out of balance with its surroundings. To clarify, reality in this perspective is each individual consciousness's assertion of ego upon the field of actuality to claim certain ideas, opinions, wants and desires which are experienced by the self. The self contains a sense of immense power, which fuels the ego, and further separates the subjective conscious disposition of an individual from everything that surrounds it in actuality. In the reality of an ego, everything does surround that one ego, ego is the type of voice of reason which states that it itself is 'the moving center of the universe' and everything that it devotes its will towards should be in relative consideration to that ego, and thusly to the self.

The formulation of the concepts above are intimately my own yet they are as well influenced by the work of two primary philosophers. The first being Ronald Bontekoe whom pursues human dignity and morality through a scientific and evolutionary perspective of man as a very intelligent animal, whom is merely an animal whose physiology and social context is adjusted for survival by following trends of evolutionary change. The second, is Fredrick Nietzsche, one of the most fantastic and articulate philosophers ever to have written. I appreciate the degree to which this book is my own creation yet I fell as though the opening lines of Nietzsche's work entitled *On Truth and Lies in a Nonmoral Sense (1873)* is essential to the type of conveyance I am attempting to provide in regards to the futility of the human ego.

"In some remote corner of the sprawling universe, twinkling among the countless solar systems, there was once a star on which some clever animals invented knowledge. It was the most arrogant, most mendacious minute in "world history," but it was only a minute. After nature caught its breath a little, the star froze, and the clever animals had to die. – One could invent a fable like this and still not have illustrated sufficiently how miserable, how shadowy and fleeting, how aimless and arbitrary the human intellect appears in nature. There were entities in which it did not exist, and when it has vanished once again, it will have left nothing in its wake. For the human intellect has no further task

beyond human life. Instead, it is merely human, and only its owner and producer regards it so pathetically as to suppose that it contains in itself the hinge on which the world turns. If we could communicate with a mosquito, we would learn that it, too, flies through the air with this same pathos, feeling itself to be the moving center of the entire world. There is nothing in nature so abject and lowly that it would not instantly swell up like a balloon at the faintest breath of that cognitive faculty." Freidrick Nietzsche.

Thoughts as deeply expressed as the Nietzsche quote above require much reflection, and re-reading. The effectual scope and force of this statement should be applicable to the inner thoughts of all persons. Encompassing their own feelings of inefficiency and inadequacy, the powerlessness that is the root of the heart of our *will to power*. Yet this death of the importance of the ego as expressed individually, births a new prospective of life. This new life prospective can contain a new possibility for enjoyment, a stripping of frustration towards this futility, and new hope for the re-realization of the aspect of pleasure and its play in consciousness. Good feelings are granted from good acts.

21 Juillet

We road down Semnoz on our shitty bikes, packs and all. Breaking was hard, and my rims and breaks were very hot requiring me to stop a few times to allow them to cool down in the wonderful breezes of the forest blanketing lower Semnoz. Eventually, near the bottom of the mountain, Bobby got a flat tire… we parted ways when we got to the town. I started not feeling well, from not eating enough, drinking too much, the change in altitude and physical exertion from the hot sun atop the mountain all day for the event. When I went through town alone I got lost, and accidently began coming down near L'Église and eventually I found myself entering the medieval city walls into Vielle Ville de Annecy. I went home and I could not get in. My host parents were 45 kilometers away. I threw up in the garden, overwhelmed and overstressed by this impediment upon my day's mission. I washed up and brushed my teeth with the garden hose. I then went to the café and met with Bobby, I felt tired and went to his apartment, and Bobby stayed at the café.

A Spanish girl named Elaina whom studies with us lives a floor below Bobby. I was tired, but not quite ready for sleep due to being beyond exhaustion. So I walked down the stairs and rang her bell. Elaina let me in very caringly and with much hospitality. She had little food yet tried to offer me some as she was about to eat herself. I turned it down and accepted only water, and her company in conversation. I told her the truth, I was not hungry, just very tired. At first I had tried to refuse even water. To which she replied, "Are you sure? My water is very cold," indeed it was. Too cold in fact, it was frozen and could not be poured! Luckily she had another cold bottle which was not frozen. She then had to leave to see the other Spanish students. Even though I had already entered Bobby's apartment I had not slept, and so I went to bed. Finally.

After resting I woke up, and went home, showered, packed and changed. I was smoking a spliff near the café when I saw Mathew. I yelled, "Aloha oe Bruddah, hele mai! Hele Mai!, (which is a directed aloha, come here, come here.) We smoked, met with Bobby and talked story. Mathew left to go about his business, and Bobby and I went to La Buvette du Marché.

It is market day, so the streets are filed. People rush through the tables of the café terrace. Like all, desperately trying to find their place in the world. Amidst our conversation I noticed a woman with some kind of disability came through with a cane. Coming from the other direction were two other obese women which in time were directly in her way. Due to her disability she was not very agile and she couldn't change her direction quickly enough to out maneuver them, so they had to wait for her to go by... There was a disheartening look of disgust on their faces. It seemed as though they were offended that she was disabled, and secondly in their way. Clearly she was unable to move out of their path as a result of her disability. Likely her disability is something she has limited to no control over.

What I cannot figure out is why they feel elite and act that way towards someone. The ego is often quite mysterious. Someone, whom is other than themselves, and has trials and difficulties that they in their own subjective stream can never fully comprehend. I think as well that even if you were able to understand someone else's disposition entirely, you would likely dislike what you find about yourself from their eyes. You would not wish upon yourself the difficulties that the other person finds in their own operating and psycho-emotional status. Even now, I have trouble comprehending all of the intricacies of my own consciousness; I suppose that all in all I am just as silly as anyone else.

A la Plage, Annecy

I road my bike from the café, feeling still nearly completely exhausted, to the shores of the lake just outside of Centre-Ville. As the time has gone by on my journey I realize more and over that I do not know where I am or what I am doing. I do not know anymore because I myself am lost. With so much constantly changing all around me as I attempt to soak it all in, I am overwhelmed, it would be easier to choose ignorance but I am on a quest for new knowledge. I search and search endlessly for the truth, for happiness, and for comfort. Yet in actuality, I am searching for something which I am not sure exists. Is there a constant state that can be achieved? Truth, so relative I doubt we will ever have access to it. Happiness so fleeting that I doubt it can be eternally achieved. Comfort equally as fleeting as happiness. Am I stuck in moments which I can at very most soak in and enjoy for what they are, never able to construct through my life anything greater than a loose conscious conglomeration of memories and feelings of past moments which alter the way I perceive whatever is happening around me in new now moments. And in the end, what is it that I find as a result of this? I find nothing, nothing more than what I always had had, everything.

Retourner á La Buvette

The café tonight is loud. Le Tour de France is over, and as a result there are all kinds of strange energies in the air. There is a subtle but vibrant electricity emanates from the different people and tourists as they circulate through the streets of la Ville-Ville du Annecy. This kind of diversity, and resonance I have found nowhere else.

Often times here I feel trapped in a world I can only understand so much of. A prisoner of English in a French prison. Where to go, and what to do, and also with who? Life and philosophy constantly propose themselves as one big question, with both none and many answers. My answer today will likely be different than tomorrow's or than someone else's on any given day. Maybe I benefit from getting lost in order to further my search for wisdom, it takes me to the knowledge I did not previously know existed. I should find more time to be confused and scared, and I will in the madness find some parts of myself which had until now ben missing. If, I cannot find these parts that does not mean that they do not exist, just that I, for whatever reason, cannot see them from my current perspective. The world hides things from me, and I hide things from myself as well. As we both create and validate our own existences, I and the world.

What is this insatiable thirst? A seemingly perpetual lack of contentment. Café after café I drink and drink while the world around me changes and changes not. I find myself only and always wanting more. Others as well plagued by their own human existence, always wanting and waiting for more.

Regeneration

Newness is not only paramount to creativity but it also functions as an important aspect to our conscious computations. Every day we wake up to a new day, the world resets itself and we have all new experiences. Even if you go to the same places, and see the same people, and undergo what seems relatively to be the same tasks they are all different than they were in the past. These new moments bring with them changes ushered into a seemingly familiar situation. Each idea, thought, reaction, and emotion is a new and unique occurrence. There is an illusion that things are not new because they are familiar. Even things which are familiar are new and in our perceptions there-of we are taking in new information and encoding things slightly differently than they were the day before. Do we not sit with the same friends in the same places and carry on different conversations. Or go to the same place with different persons, or with the same persons to different places. In these situations there are some aspects which are highly familiar to our recollection of past events, yet because there is some physical change the metaphysical weight of the instance undergoes differentiation and change as well.

Each day the grass grows, and the sun is in a different

position as are the entire cosmos! We can tap into the nature of the regenerative spirit and use it to moderate our acceptance of our experience. When we feel uncomfortable about a new experience we can remind ourselves that they are just beautiful forms of regeneration. That change and flux are occurring before our very eyes and thusly are finding their way into our conscious subjective experience. We may be subject to change, yet we can make change beautiful if we undergo the conscious perception shifts necessary to re-encode regenerative information in a positive light. We can re-establish many of our cognitive associations that previously were negative through the regenerative spirit of nature as new positive associations. This ideologically can commence as soon as we begin to realize that the experiences of the past have faded away into our memories. They exist there to provide us with important survivorship benefits. Yet, acceptance of newness prepares us for every new moment. Essentially it is the regenerative spirit which brings us closer towards our conceptions of the pre-future.

Lemons?

21 Juillet

More lemons please! I need more lemons! We demand and we demand but how can we give ourselves? How can we give up those things we want and see the world for exactly what it is and not only for what we so desperately want it to be?

Au Lac ce Soir

An endless search for wants, for needs- for meaning. What is the difference between a want and a need if the want is necessary for one's happiness? Is that not good enough criterion to qualify as a need as well? What more could we need than to be happy and enjoy our life experience. We should at least be able to connect with others and share the joys of life. Not to be locked away and confined, in a prison of our own minds. Life is weird. It always has been, will be, and certainly there no escape but death- and no need to search for the escape until it finds us. There is in existence just endless searching, wanting and the associated confusion. Confused and alone, or confused together? I am not sure which of the two is easier, or which is more preferable, these answers change from person to person, time to time, and place to place. What is the difference anyways except for a feeling of security that temporarily exists? This temporary feeling of security exists until life or the world or the weight there-of becomes overwhelming. Shattering our weak conceptions of existence, and sweeping us and what we were up slowly with the passage of time: moving moments, they are always changing; this does not change, and it does not stop. As the great Heraclitus said, "The only thing constant is change".

I am more lost than ever, yet I am exactly where I wanted to be. But I do not know why, nor where it is that I wanted to be. Now liberated from the confines of my ego and of my past memories, they are of no use to me here in this state. I can go where I could not before, everywhere and nowhere. No longer stuck in what had been, I find myself, lost in where I am, in the moment. The sounds of the city which were so intense this morning have dulled. Peace takes over. The occasional couple on a stroll quietly passes me by as I sit on a bench along the shore of Lac Annecy. The couple strolling by was remarkably quiet in conversation, as the waves gently lap against the side of the lake. I hear a man whistle for his barking dog. Together they shatter the silence and stillness of the summer night moment. Yet, through these minor disturbances, life in the moment is peaceful.

22 Juillet

I left the house late tonight; it is Monday so the streets are relatively empty. La Buvette Du Marche is closed. So I was going to go smoke and ponder along the canal further into town. Two young guys were sitting on a bench overlooking the canal. They were both born in Chamonix, France yet live and work in Geneva, Switzerland. They asked me if I had a cigarette for them. I gladly rolled them each their own. We had a fascinating conversation about medical problems in France and in the United States. They were very kind and intelligent. However, partway through our conversation two S.D.F.'s (sans domicile fixée, or 'homeless persons') approached, and interrupted my conversation.

Interruptions

Interruptions play deeply into our expectations. When we are projecting an expected chain of actions and reactions and some external factor to those previously considered enter our processing we experience a delay in our sensations of cognitive efficiency. These interruptions are not so much by their nature interruptions, rather they are perceived as interruptions as they impede upon our conscious flow, yet are in fact working mechanisms of the actual world- mechanisms which by their introduction into our conscious stream seem to propose a problem, mainly a problem of exceeding what was previously conceived to be a possibility. Cognitive readjustment is difficult, especially in the moment. In hind sight it is easy to comprehend how we should have processed things differently, however in action we are removed by time from the comforts of the reflective process. We must rely on our emotions and vibrations to channel reactions and appropriate reactions rather than being privy to utilizing the fullness of our cognition.

The thin line between ideology and effective action is always being danced with when actuality interrupts our ideological projected reality. We are humbled at these moments, when we recognize the effects and power of not only our own mind and internal cognitive activity but also that of those whom surround us- of those other minds, and of the universe itself. I think it would be boring to be the supreme conscious intellect of the universe, never being wrong and never being caught off guard. The necessary balance between effective self-confidence and the necessities of participation in social humility should be achieved through rotations of attention between the two In some instances self-confidence is the precedent, and in other cases it is humility, it is not either or, black or white. These rotations are affectively the processing and motivating of rotations of cognitive attention towards the power of the self, and respect for the powers of others. When these transitions run smoothly we should feel little strife, and more overall effectiveness in the actual world. We will feel liberated from the interruptive impediments of the actual world, and find the happy freedom that is correctly making and applying associations of data in real time.

I do not think that the S.D.F.'s knew that I understand French. The jest of their conversation went as follows, "Hello... how are you? We have been looking all over town for something to steal so we can get some money." They said to the two French men I had been speaking with, "He has a bike, a phone, cigarettes, etc. He is an American so he must have money." At this point my two new friends replied, "No he is cool, do not mess with him." The S.D.F. then directly approached me. His face just inches from mine as he shook my hand. He was trying to intimidate me. I could not help but glance at the scar stretching from his forehead, across his left eye, and halfway down his check. After I shook hands with and speaking mundanely to the more gruesome of the two he turned stated to them again that he wanted to steal my bike. I hoped that they were not serious as I have never heard a robbery vocalized and planned out in such a manner in my entire life. I figured it was a good time to leave. Before they had a chance to attempt to do something stupid I bid them all goodnight and road off, completely weirded out, and feeling pity for them.

I then met with Bobby and his friend at the Irish pub in Annecy, Fin Kelly's. We were later joined by another student from Spain whom was also in my class. We were later as well joined by a girl to whom Bobby had taken a liking. She had arrived with two of her friends as well. We stayed at the bar and I drank coffee and water while they ordered beers. We left at closing. The Spanish students went home and Bobby and I left with the Russian girls to walk them home. Their dormitory was around the lake and clear across town. Bobby and Anastasia walk quickly and far in front of us, so I stayed back with Margaritta and Ritta cracking jokes and singing silly songs to keep them amused during the long walk. They then asked me to tell them stories. They are a fun audience and giggle a lot. As I much enjoy telling stories it was a fun night, despite what happened earlier along the canal, it was by this point long forgotten.

23 Juillet

When I woke up today I felt different. I felt as though things had changed. I felt once more like myself! Perhaps it was my sense of humor that saved me through the awkwardness of the previous evening. I knew that if the man tried to steal my bike I likely would have tried to pick him up and throw him into the canal; in the moment it would have been the most sensible option. Or maybe it was the satisfaction of sharing my ridiculous stories. I knew that today was going to be a good day; I was right! Class went well and afterwards Bobby arranged for a restaurant to hold a film screening, fully catered with food, wine, and desert. It was overall a very successful event. Bobby is good at arranging social outings and events, very Dutch…

You can never be sure where you or anyone will end up in life. So enjoy the interruptions, enjoy the variety that exists while you are alive; because in the long run it is true to say that life is short.

24 Juillet

Is it only possible to think about something in the past? This question causes me to ponder the concept of a 'momentary existence'. It does seem as though we can only think about things in the past, although we are always living in the present. The time delay between perception and processing, though very brief, seems to be the factor which makes it impossible to think about the present moment fully. As well, thoughts about the future are not really about the actual future. They are only our projections of our expectations. The mind, as quick as it is, cannot be actively processing the actual moment at hand. Our programmed reactions and emotions carry us through moments of being. We seem to be trapped and confused. Being unable to cognitively access actuality, we need to wait and let our minds sift through it into our streams of accessible reality- and this takes time.

I think that 'now' is always the present moment; our reflections of the past are only our reflections upon the fragments we were able to perceive. Furthermore, only the fragments which our memory has encoded from those experiences recorded as information which was fed into us from our base perceptual modes. We are surely then always intellectually confused and constantly reacting with uncomforting emotions as we sort the past into the past, and formulate our predictions about the future.

Cognitive Distancing

It should by now be apparent how the mind distances and isolates itself from other objects and persons via instating the ego into the conscious stream. However, the distances inserted by cognition are not always those of physical space, but can also be distances in time and metaphysical comprehension. It is impossible for any human being to be present the time at which their parents first met. To view the gaze between their eyes, and to sense the pheromones emitted, the energy vibrations that were to begin a chain leading to their own existence. They do not understand this part of existence which led to their existence, yet they experience it when they experience themselves. We through our cognitive existences are forced to be distanced through time. This is an important factor in the cognitive distancing between momentary experience and cognitive reflection.

Time and space may be conquered by the mind according to some postulations, but perhaps this conquering as well can only be through the medium of time and space. Requiring distance from the actual occurrence for the conquering to take place, and it requires time for the processing and reflection to occur. Just where we are now, is at least one step or more removed from everything and everywhere else at all times, because of change as a constant.

A Commencer Ce Soir

25 Juillet

I have been sitting here at the beach for hours, thinking, processing, and attempting to draw my consciousness closer to the present. Attempting to guide my consciousness towards the kind of future that I think I want. But always there is another choice, another possible reality looming on the other end of every decision. If I spend all of my time in calculation, speculation, and consideration do I not as a side effect inevitably dive into the past, drawing my thoughts farther and farther with every passing moment from the actuality of now. I draw away from self-realization, and into a functioning of airy thoughts and unrealistic ideology. The kind of thoughts external to social reality, a continuous process of being wrong and not being presently present.

We are and always will be haunted by the past. Followed by ghosts of the things we have seen and the things we have done- the phantoms of our memories. These hauntings are intimate as they originate in our own experiences and the things we think we have known. Our past pours itself into our expectations, and into our processing of the present. From this, from time, we cannot hide. We all are its prisoners serving our sentences. Living in this sense is a waiting to die, amidst our confusion, our processing, and our discomfiture with our own existences.

I digress, philosophy itself is liberating, and it is the attempt, the honest attempt at understanding and attempting to apply that understanding towards right action. For a few moments after writing this I laughed at the idea; the idea of aimlessly waiting to die, and filling that time with anything less than the best thoughts. It seemed miserable to submit to that type of existence. This must be why often times perceived misery brings about the enactment my sense of humor. The point of the adventure, the point of the march, is to always continue onwards with positivity.

A stranger sits in a foreign place. Uncomfortable and unable to communicate as she wishes- she clings, she holds on tight to whatever she thinks will return comfort upon her. So she moves, and moves again. Each new spot is uncomfortable at first. She longs for what she just left, what she is as of just now finally able to understand. Now that she has distanced her mind from the actuality of its existence, she can really understand it. Throughout her life she traverses from place to place, across time, adjusting and trying to form new conceptions of the term 'understanding', her endless quest.

Part Seven

FEAR AND LIBERATION

Fear and Liberation

I am already swimming deep with no sight of land, so I might as well keep going and see what there is to see. The introspective depth into the human consciousness offered by philosophy has roots that extend far into the past. They stem from other languages and cultures forgotten and eroded by the winds of time. The attempts to understand both the world around us and our cognitive play in phenomenological events stretches back farther than the creation of systems of writing. It is complicated to track anything down to its original source. So many have influenced so many others, and the works which survived are the only indications we have to attribute ideas to persons, periods, and regions. One of the most influential ancient philosophers for modern philosophy of mind, existentialism, phenomenology, and pragmatics is Plato. Mainly I am speaking of a selection from Plato's *Republic book VII* which plays heavily into these themes.

For those of you unfamiliar with this passage this is more famously referred to as Plato's 'Allegory of the Cave'. In The Republic book VII work we find the basic structuring of human programing as offered by the apparent world which exists inside the cave, as well as the play of imagination, discovery, cognition, and the futility of truth sharing and effective communication of phenomenon. A sufficient summery of the Allegory of the Cave is as follows;

There are humans whom dwell in an underground cave; there is an entrance from which the light of the outside world peers in. The humans have dwelled here since "childhood", more specifically since infancy. Their bodies are chained to a wall such that they are unable to move either their legs or their heads. Above and behind them is a fire, and between this fire and the wall to which they are chained is a pathway. Along this pathway persons carry figures such as "vessels, statues and figures of animals made of wood and stone and various materials". These figures illuminated by the fire cast shadows upon the wall the prisoners are gazing at. As the puppets move across the walkway, the prisoners observe and encode the information (shadows) that they perceive. This is the rational basis for all of the prisoners' knowledge. As Plato wrote, "how could they see anything but the shadows if they were never allowed to move their heads?" To which one could simply reply, that they cannot, this is the entirety of their reality.

Furthermore, because they are still benefit as humans to language, they can converse with one another and have names for the figures which pass before them. They can discuss, and recall in a commutative fashion what it is that they are experiencing. Because of this there is a shared perspective of what reality is, and what in the past has constituted as reality, namely the progression of shadowy figures projected onto the wall in front of them.

Now suppose that one of the prisoners is somehow freed, he sees the other prisoners chained, the pathway and the figures being carried along it, as well as the fire, and also off in the distance he can see the light coming in from the entrance to the cave. He would naturally wander towards the light at the mouth of the cave, and be blinded by it. He begins to gather that what he had been seeing his entire life was an illusion, and that what he was seeing now was the truth. Will he be bewildered and wish to return to the safety of his primary conception of reality? Even though he now may walk and see more than he has ever seen before, he will eventually at some point want to return to the reality of cognition in which the objects that he has seen his entire life are truer than the reality he is now being exposed to and must now confront cognitively.

The light beaming in from the entrance to the cave will pain him both physically as he is not used to light of such intensity, but also cognitively as he has no prepared associations for what sight may bring his mind along with the new light. He will be blind for a temporal period of time- as he adjusts physically, emotionally, and cognitively to the newness of reality that is surrounding him, and in fact flowing around him and trying to flow into and through his mind. Eventually he brings himself out of the mouth of the cave and is confronted with the sun in all its magnificence for the very first occasion in his entire life.

"Clearly he would first see the sun, and then reason about him." He would first experience things in their new-ness, and his cognition would be running full speed yet always just behind trying to sort and process reactions to these new stimuli. Those other prisoners left in the cave have absolutely none of this new knowledge he has gained. Would he then wish to return to those old forms of knowl-edge, those old ideas which he now knows are not the full and complete actuality of existence? Or would he reason that in this new light, this new truth, it would be better to, "be the poor servant of a poor master, and to endure anything, rather than think as they do and live after their manner?" This notion that Plato is conveying here is that it is better to suffer knowing the truth and confronting it, than it would be to shield oneself from the truth because it is more comfortable than existential examination of new truths.

He is alone in this feat; no other prisoner with whom he has shared community and life would understand his new sensations and ideas. In fact, the potential of sharing his ideas can be completely harmful pragmatically to his existence. He may face shunning, a lack of potential inter-actions, and even the loss of his own life. This severity was not excluded from Plato's allegory, "Men would say of him that up he went and down he came without his eyes; and that it was better not even to think of ascending; and if any one tried to loosen another and lead him up to the light, let them only catch the offender, and they would put him to death." Not only is his experience uncommunicable as it is so uniquely his own, but it is also un-sharable in that he cannot convince others to try to create a replica of it in their own lives, and of their own experience and process-ing there-of. Essentially he cannot bring anyone else to his light, or else he will have to face rejection, and that no one wishes for.

This perhaps is the reason why most people never venture too far from shore or too far from home. They are scared of what they will find; terrified that it will shatter all of their previous conventions of existence. That all the knowledge gathered and distributed by their societal ancestors will be in vain, and that they will forsake their own identity if they seek out these new truths. We all have emotional attachments that keep us clinging onto the past, and to the perceived consciousness's' of others. These emotional bonds seem unbreakable, yet in fact they are quite fragile and that is why so much emotional effort is naturally asserted to protect them. They are vulnerable, they may be interrupted at any time, and thus we are fearful of their disappearance, and fearful of what this emotional unsettling will mean for the rest of our lives. Many would rather return to the shadows and lock themselves in to the comfort of their previous normality than to venture out of the cave.

The ideas I would like to stress are a dichotomy that is derived from this Allegory. The dichotomy I wish to highlight is that of fear and of liberation. The emotional stress which compels us to stay with comfort and normality is represented by the possibility of chaining oneself back down into the cave, to continue one's life avoiding the light. Effectively this is a conscious choice towards ignorance, towards ignoring the newness and possibility of there being more to actuality than what rests in one's previously constituted conceptualization of reality.

What will we choose? Would we rather venture out into unfamiliar territory or hide where we know what we know is 'known' by others? Do we dare to take those essential first steps towards the realization of our potential for liberation? I hope so, as difficult as it may be, even life consuming. I think if I must suffer existential pains in life I would rather do it living a life of suffering in the truth, than aimlessly and tiringly living in the darkness and falsity.

We may paint our ideas of the world such that they may be pleasing to us; and of those paintings which bring about pain, we in our human nature generally tend to attempt to ignore them. What if some pains are good? What if some of them must occur precursory to the greatest achievement of pleasure? We cannot be certain either way, and when it comes to survival and the pursuit of happiness it is best for us to make that jump. If we jump with true and honest intentions then we know that we have the ability to jump and jump again as it becomes necessary. It appears as well that this is the kind of liberty that may be best for the prisoner. That he may jump back and forth between the world of darkness and the world of light. So that when one is not fulfilling and vivid enough or the other is too frightening he may be where he chooses when he chooses, that he may be free to make this choice without severe social or emotional impediment.

Yet these obstacles, our desires and fears, we place before ourselves. We make it such that we ourselves have to deal with them. They are not the assertions of the world, but our assertions upon the world. That because of our perspective it must be either this way or that. Are things so black and white? Perhaps inside of the cave things are black and white, yet in the world exterior to the cave there is a full spectrum of color, even those colors beyond the human's evolutionary capabilities to perceive. There is always more and there is always another newness waiting to be discovered, if only we can get over our fear and our self-asserted blockages we may eventually find this new light, the new truth, and more fullness of reality. The more we fear, the less liberty we have. The less we fear the more liberty we have.

Questions and Disputes of Self Realization

Existence is vast- It so easily may encompass either fear or liberation. We are left here to contemplate our own existences in the deepest sense of existentialist thought. Questions which arise are such as; Does it matter if humans live lost and scare inside the cave of ignorance, so long as they are still happy doing so? Also is it possible for unhappiness to live outside of the cave? In the light of the sun, does the sun not temporarily fade away and leave us lost and scared? If we view people in the cave whom believe they are seeing reality, is someone watching us in a stream of infinite greater regression of observers and contemplators- or are we the highest level of observation? Is there something more real than perceptual reality? And if there is should we think about that which is unperceivable? We can never know if we are right about something we can't perceive because we have no means of measuring it for analysis and communicative comparison. Can we be liberated from the chain which we have learned existence and philosophy adhere to? That existence leads to choices, choices lead to possibility of right and or wrong actions, which leads us to the necessity of ethical formulations, and eventually the sum total of all these calculations still results in the death of the individual and the uncertainty of that which follows or accompanies death.

It must be much easier to exist within the cave than to

exist where I suppose that I myself sit-outside of the cave on a rock, questioning life under a tree, gazing up at reality and the enormity of the sun. It is nothing other than ignorance which forms the walls of the cave. It is better to dance with others around the tree, because together we can battle the weather. We can aid and comfort each other, though we exist on our own journeys we have so much to learn from each other. I question now what then is the difference between unknowingness and ignorance? I would postulate that unknowingness seems to be a lack of capacity for determined choice, while ignorance is a conscious action. One can as well walk the line between the two. If one is ignorantly unknowing they are rejecting their capacity for knowing which drives them into unknowing ignorance. Yet, one whom is only unknowing has no capacity for making decisions. In common terms we refer to both as ignorance. This unknowing individual has no determined choice towards ignorance and is simply unknowing.

In this the unknowing person is still locked into their chains, and has never heard of the possibility of freedom, this individual may be pitied by others, but they are so unaware of this great intricacy that they are unaware even of the pity they are receiving. The other whom is knowingly ignorant has perhaps been freed, or heard the recantation of one whom has been freed, and has still made a consciously decisive effort to remain ignorant contradictive to evidence of true knowledge.

How can we determine when it is good then for our existence or for our cognition to choose to be ignorant (if ever)? Only by knowing can we know when to appropriately approach and utilize the powers of ignorance. It appears trying to use ignorance to conscious advantage is self-defeating to the pursuit of knowledge. Ignorance in its pure sense of truth lacking then only applies to the persons unaware of their own ignorance, whom are thusly un-knowingly ignorant. And knowing-full ignorance is a deviance which occurs when someone wishes for oneself to be ignorant rather than to acknowledge their knowing as a result of choice and conscious action. This is of course a method applied when the individual appeals that he has something to gain as a result of at least issuing the appearance of 'being' unknowingly ignorant; a feat in which the goal is more to appear ignorant than to actually be ignorant as knowing-full ignorance is as I have stated is self-contradictory. This type of knowing-full ignorance is an illusory lie.

In order to determine these degrees of ignorance and knowing we must somehow gather a sufficient definition for what knowing is. Is it an intrinsic feeling, or is it something that we create logical sureness about? It is ironic that we are more likely to emotionally perceive the intimate feeling of knowing something more-so than we are able to convince others that we know that we know something. Perhaps Socrates was correct in his assertions that no one really knows anything, they are really just thinking about it and applying through rhetoric the assertions they wish to imply to be knowledge without having an actual essential foundation as truth. Is then, knowing even possible aside from emotion and the feelings of knowingness? Is that not what a world of devices, computers and robots wishes to achieve? Humanlike qualities of intellect without the impediments of emotion into the calculating process…

If we cannot know, we are forcibly unknowingly ignorant by our human natures, just as it is the nature of the prisoners to be chained to the wall in the state which they exist. What then is it to know? Are there levels of knowing? Science, math, history, spirituality and the like all seem to be fields but not levels of knowing. Perhaps this attempt at dividing knowledge drops the mind off in the right place- as an assortment of knowing, and not a hierarchy. And if we undergo the division by placing any segment of the assortment as a representative of the mean, between knowing and not knowing we create balance. This balance can be a cognitive thought space in which our minds can exist with peace, and through the peace and stillness we may find temporary pleasure from cognitive equilibrium.

If we can be free, we can enter and exit knowing and the feeling of knowing at will, because we have learned to identify the differences between the two perceptual modes. Those who are not free, are they in said condition by choice? Whether they do this knowingly or unknowingly, I do not know.

To dance is to be free, to reject ones confines and to make a path through the labyrinth of existence and of experience. So be free and you will be free to know your own mode of knowing and to dance and to live as you choose. You will still be confused as to the next note, and as to the rhythm a new beat, but having the confidence to move regardless of your unknowingness is the key to progression, the key to efficiency in movement, eventually by nature you will begin to move, pragmatically in the knowingness of your own derived truths in relation to the world of actuality- ideologically speaking. I think I think I know enough to think I am knowing-fully free, and by that I mean that I am aware of my confines. At the very least I feel that I am free to know that I think I know I am free.

Our freedom will come and go like the ebb and flow

of time. We will be free enough to utilize it cognitively at times, yet at other times we will be buried in emotions, and buried in the perceived instabilities of life. Rose bushes through their stems form a bud, and the buds bloom. As we are then able to appreciate their beauty for some time, the beautiful rose eventually fades away and disintegrates in front of us. It disintegrates so that it may spread its vitality, and again find itself in the recourse of existence. Either as a rose or as something else, its energy and its matter does not flow out of existence. It merely shifts shapes, and changes itself as it is pressed upon the hinges of its own existence and as it becomes that which it becomes as it becomes that which it becomes. And in the moment of its' 'isness' it is what it is, unknowable, primary to cognition. It lays in waiting for us to come about as cognitive beings to uncover its truth yet again.

If all things are always changing knowledge then is not absolute, it is not static, and it is not 'concrete'. Static conceptions of knowledge are missing the cognitive mean of thought, evading adjustable virtue of knowledge and its potential applications for existence. It is in some respect the potentiality of becoming the confines which force us to knowingly enter into a guise of ignorance as a feeble attempt to regain the emotions of security we equate as necessary in regards to the preservation of our freedom. We may again be wise to listen to the lessons played out be Socrates, and only think that we might know something; rather than to knowingly, but wrongfully assert it as absolute and universally communicable knowledge. I can adjust to a life only thinking that I know, as long as I know that I think.

The Spectrum of the Mind

There are times when we do not feel ourselves. Our being is still intact, yet we feel different than what we would identify as 'normal'. I think that our energy channels at these times are blocked or perhaps open but feel different because they are normally blocked and the usual sense of balance between ego and being which create our sense of normalcy is exaggerated out of equilibrium. The feelings of normalcy and malaise are both subject to go through fluctuations of change. We will find ourselves cycling in and out of equilibrium, excess, and blockages.

What we call normal is very likely that which is habitual. We say it is normal to wake up at a certain time, or to eat certain foods, to commit certain actions, these are normal to us because they are our habits. They are deeply encoded into the individual's psyche, the thoughts and their corresponding actions are highly developed neural pathways. When the pathways already established are utilized, there is a corresponding hormonal approval or disapproval. What are most habitual are animal instincts, mainly the drives towards food, shelter, sleep, and sex.

Animals that live in the wild can be skittish to say the least. They often only come around humans when food is involved, whether the food is being offered or not. When an animal calculates that it is worth the risk of going near a human in order to obtain food, it is hunger and the ego's hunger for survival which encourages the animal to go beyond its normal risk taking programing, making it intensely self-assertive towards obtaining the food source.

In these instances, hormonal instincts are flooding the mind of the animal telling it that its need for food, the pleasure associated with the fulfillment of this hunger, and furthermore the associated pragmatic benefit of survival are greater than the risks associated with the reward. There is a hidden aspect to cognition; much of the subconscious mind operates off of a non-linguistic mode of cognition which functions to process our memories, social programing, and hormone secretion in order to calculate perceived potential possibilities for risk/reward and loss/gain. Once these calculations are completed the animal reacts by projecting its expectations of receiving the previously mentioned benefits upon the physical world through its actions in attempt to utilize that potential benefit, this occurs subconsciously. Of course we humans are none different- only in that we quite consciously and cognitively think about things, though we do not always think before we act.

In our metaphysical thought spaces we create and explore systems using symbols. I think that the basis for our creative and imaginary powers rely heavily upon our social programing; what is given to us is what we first have to work with. When we wander from the ideas of others and begin to think of our own ideas we in our explorations experience certain ideas, objects, or images which alter hormonal secretions and brain wave energy emissions from the state of 'normalcy'. We begin feeling different and find ourselves no longer to be the selves that we thought or had projected ourselves to be; meaning that we find ourselves not as the previously constituted ideological self but as the actual self- or the self as it actually is. We then rearrange our thoughts and feel compulsion to usher these ideas and the feelings they invoke into linguistic formatting. The meaning of our intended message is carried loosely through the conveyance of these arranged symbols which we call language, and the audience reflects upon possible meanings which can be derived from the pattern of linguistic symbols encoded. Each individual audience processes the message relative to the contextual field of reference that they have available.

We may like to think that we think before we feel things. However, in order to think about something we must rely on our primary sensations. Our metaphysics are relative to the physical context. Our feelings from these sensations are hormonally recognized and this creates an electric storm of thoughts, and then those thoughts reverberate and influence the overall perception of sensation. Simply put once perception of something is initiated we are then able to think about it; and since the cognitive aspects are secondary, we are always subject firstly to the actual situation as first felt by our sensations, and secondly to the logical symbolic allowances of that sense information as it becomes available to our cognitive processing. Thusly once-more, we are always one step removed from physics by our own interpretations of metaphysics.

What I believe this means for the psycho-emotional spectrum is that in times of panic, where our cognitive functions are suppressed we are more likely to react emotionally, as we feel the situation is substantially out of our cognitive realm of control. Persons whom commit crimes, unless subject to mental illness, usually only commit these crimes because of their need for survival. Such as the man whom discussed stealing my bike and belongings along the canal in France. He if he had no *need* to be out on a night of theft he would have been occupied and have his intellect applied to some area other than prospecting goods to steal; if he so had the lack of a need to survive pressuring him to attempt to commit crimes which one without the hyper stressed spectrum would not feel so compelled to undergo.

I recognize that unfortunately despite our great intellects and conscious wills we humans can and will be at moments pushed by the stresses and needs for survival to do things commonly thought to be contrary to humanity. It is not that humanity the metaphysical concept is failing because of the occurrence of any of these particular instances of violation of social codes for survival prospects, merely that humanity in some sense is surviving because it is willing to accept risks. Some might argue about occurrences of 'crimes against humanity' from the perspective of the existence of evil. One could argue that there are 'simply evil' people whom exist, and that these evil people habitually preform evil deeds. I rather prefer to speculate that some the people whom preform deeds which are by some referred to as 'evil' are actually pressured by their environment or at least are perceiving to be actually pressured by their environment towards being compelled to preform acts of 'evil'. Yet, I suppose I could as well accept that there are a few evil people out there, whom are just hell bent on destruction.

I in my ethical ponderings prefer to not refer to instances of fights for survival amongst evolutionary beings as evil. I see the un-ethicality or the 'evil' as arising only when surplus of survival need is involved- and one commits malicious acts for the pleasure of the action. Their neural pathways have been designed to offer pleasure at the pain of others; it is when one harms others for the pleasure of harming them in which we find valid characteristics of something to which I would agree to call evil being displayed.

This play between logical need-action processing is not limited to severe cases and crimes; through pragmatic vision these modules of thought action relations play a pivotal role in many day to day experiences. Why did the chicken cross the road you ask? Likely, the chicken crossed the road because it perceived some kind of benefit whether survival based or pleasure based in crossing the road. There will be instances in which chickens miscalculate the prospects of crossing roads (just as humans do from time to time), and the chicken is ran over, or runs into the mouth of a predator in waiting. Likely, there will be a multitude of instances in which the chicken makes the crossing safely. If the subjective introspection of the chicken saw no prospective gains in crossing the road, the attempt of road crossing would never have been undergone regardless of whether or not the chicken makes it safely across the road- because the motivation of survival or pleasure benefit are not weighty enough to compel the chicken to cross the road.

We will continue repeating certain actions so long as we receive either A) survival benefit or B) pleasure from carrying out the action. There are often cases in which there is a pleasure gained, but when the pleasure gains begin to interrupt survival benefit, in time the actions will realign with that which provides a higher risk of survival benefit, and the motivational drive towards higher pleasure rewards begin to be struck down. Our memories form a barrier to help save us from these self-damaging habituations. This argument could be applied to a vast array of instances, and I believe comprehension of what I am trying to express here provides an interesting perspective into the psycho-emotional spectrum, its influence on our feelings, cognitive reactions, and physical actions, and habituation there of in an evolutionary psychological framework.

28 Juillet

I have not taken the time to write lately, because I have been too busy living. I think this is a very good excuse for my procrastination! I blame Sarah. She is classy and sophisticated, wise yet holds true to the spirit of adventure, beautiful and chic, her sense of style is truly magnificently French and slightly noir. I have in the midst of my studies and life here been enjoying that I have been feeling myself and very comfortable around her. She only becomes more interesting to me in lieu of our shared interests in art, philosophy, literature, film, music, and all of the intellectual feats of existence which I as well believe make life as a human worth living and enjoyable.

A few days ago we had our first date, we rented a pedal boat and cruised around the lake, and had a glass of rosé at a lakeside bar. It was nice to get away from all of the other students and the microclimate of our social circles and to spend some time with someone completely removed from that entire realm which I found myself in the midst of. I recall riding home afterwards on my bike feeling alive and very content with this new connection. Last night Sarah invited me to a party along the lake with music, games, drinks, and high spirits certainly filled the air. I reveled in my reflection that the entire soiree pétanque tournament was so very French and I found the stimulation from this newness was wonderful. I road home on my bike again- This time in the rain, and again content with my experience, satisfied with this human connection.

I awoke today with a smile. I swam well through my dreams last night. I am on my way to meet Sarah again. I love to allow myself to be distracted by love affairs, inside of me lives a true romantic. On my way to meet her I stopped at the café for coffee and to write. I felt we were lucky to spend another lovely day together. She is to me very mysterious and a little dark, yet fantastic company especially because of my interest in her intellect.

Diner at home was sensational as usual; my host mother is such a fantastic cook. She and her husband used to own their own restaurant in which she was the only chef. She would cook dinner and lunch for hundreds of persons every single day. Alas now that I was dining in their home and she was retired she cooks for only the three of us. I feel so blessed to have a different three course meal every evening, and not to mention that she often crafts her own deserts!

I am completely immersed in a world of newness, everything here is different than anywhere else I have been and anything I have previously experienced. I find myself now pondering how different is different? It certainly is not the same. Yet, if it is the same, it is still different. I am going to have to learn to be okay with different sameness, and the same differences in life. Since everything is always changing, I must.

30 Juillet

Shortly after Bobby, our Russian friends and I left the café that night, there was a storm, rain pouring down forming a small river coursing through the old cobblestone streets of Annecy. Lightning flashes illuminated the sky, the Alps, and the town as loud bursts of thunder rolled through the streets. I then found myself standing across from the now closed cafe under some shelter with Bobby, Ritta, Margaritta, and Anastasia. I was smoking a cigarette and coordinating our passages home. On a usual night Bobby and I would walk them back to the dormitories with our bikes in hand. After bringing them safely home we would ride through the town together and split ways at a traffic circle to go to our own homes. Tonight it was raining far too hard to make the usual journey. In the midst of our coordinating a taxi ride for the girls I noticed the approach of the very same SDF whom just a few days ago had discussed stealing my bike. He was drunk and dirty as usual.

He asked me for a cigarette which I rolled and gave him despite my abundant despise for him. He then offered me wine from his bag (not a bottle, but a bag). I took some because I felt that in order to be polite I had no other choice but to play his game. I say this in that I believe in decency and respecting other humans regardless of their appearance and backgrounds (regardless even of the things they have said and done). I envisioned this interaction as a chance for peace, I was not seeking his friendship but I certainly wanted to make peace with this human.

This was an incredibly different interaction than the previous night. We were on a covered walkway in this instance, a walkway which overlooked the same small park near the canal where we had encountered each other the other evening. This area is as close to home as he has. While I on the other hand have many homes, many places where I can take off my shoes or slippers and call home. For the time being I even have a home in Annecy- also my parents' home in Southern California, and Oahu my home in the middle of the sea, and the houses of many friends which I could call home if need be. This different interaction was an unexpected solution to the difficulty I faced when my human experience came intersected with his.

He asked me again for another cigarette and offered more wine in exchange. I obliged a second cigarette but told him that I had to leave because I had to take the Russian girls to a taxi that was to take them home since Bobby and I could not escort them back safely ourselves this evening on account of the storm. Everyone wanted to return to our own dwellings as quickly as possible to get out of the storm. A part of me inside struggled with knowing that he himself has no actual home. I think what I felt was more a sensation of pity than despise. Eventually I had made way for my exit from the interaction. He bid me bon soiree as I walked off to meet the taxi. I was content as some degree of peace was established.

I received a message on my phone from Sarah, informing me that she was to leave for a week because of her job. We were able to meet for drinks, and we sat at a nice café along the canal. I had never been to this café

*as sitting at La Buvette du Marche was so habitual.
We sat and talked for a while when some of her girl-
friends were walking along the canal, spotted us and
joined us for drinks. It has been such a pleasant experience to have met someone whom handles everything
with a smile and apparently abundant grace. Her
friends were funny and very kind.*

*Afterwards we went back to her girlfriend's apartment
for more music and a fantastic 2003 vintage. Spending
the evening with these three ladies was an unexpected
but welcomed twist in my plans. I reflected on this
rare and culturing experience; that even though I have
been living in France for weeks, I rarely experienced
such a natural glimpse inside of French home life at a
level which foreigners do not often have the privilege
to experience.*

*It was a refreshing reminder of the problems and in-
terests all humans share as facets of their humanity. I
am speaking of the pains and the joys, the comfort and
the discomfiture of human existence. There is such an
immense beauty to be found though not only through
traveling but the sharing of culture with the persons
you meet whilst traveling. There is no need to be shy.*

2 Août

*I left school on my bike, with sandwich supplies in my
backpack. Today instead of picnicking at the lake with
my friends or eating somewhere in town I wanted to
eat by myself. I slowed down as I road by the cemetery
which I pass every day on my way to and from school.*

The gate was open so I road on in. I made a few tours of the graves and noticed the majority had Catholic markings; a couple of Jewish graves existed as well. Then I came across a grave which had no religious markings whatsoever. I found this to be strange, there was an open spot next to that grave with no one buried in it yet. There I sat on the empty plot and made my sandwich. I enjoyed my lunch in solitude and afterwards I lay down and closed my eyes. I began to imagine death.

I began to imagine what it would be like to be a conscious entity not connected to a body and not in the material world. After a few moments of this rather absurd form of reflection I realized I should live while I am alive, and worry about death when it comes. I gathered my things, and road through the town to go and find my friends along the lake.

I think that I am thinking of life because Sartre had influenced me to think of death. I reflect upon those precious moments we humans experience, memories are just as fragile as the persons we share them with. One moment they are next to you experiencing the same event from their own perspective and the next moment they can be gone. We may not always have consciously controlled play in the moments we encounter, but each individual has a degree of discernment towards their intentions. Furthermore, it is in our reflections when we choose the sentiment that we wish to hold in regards something which has happened. We effectively form our own memories and sentimental degrees of attachment towards persons, objects, and experiences. All of this conscious play however exists only in hindsight; it exists in our recollection and reflection of lived experience.

The freedom to paint our own perspective of the world apparently only exists for the living soul, what though of the dead? What of those whom pass holding a lifetime of personal and intimate memories. Do they and their memories pass as quickly as the moments they are formed after? I suppose that it is impossible to know until one is dead, and even then it is even more impossible to know. For now all that I can know is that I think that life is weird, and I am slowly convincing myself to think that weirdness is okay.

If we choose what we choose because we choose it, how do we arrive at our spectrum of possible present conscious choices? It seems as though our choices arrive at our consciousness based off of a synthesis of random chance (effects upon us) and our previous choices (our past record of effects upon things and stuff). We will suffer if we remain in a state of living in ignorance or fear. Living in such doubt would cause us to fail to recognize the power of wills that we do have. We may accidentally enslave ourselves and loose the possibility of our free agency. We may become slaves to some other entity; whether it is money, power, evolution, love, or even our own memories. We can so easily fall into many forms of slavery becoming subject to our own ignorance and our own fears, leaving the possibility of choice behind the moment we chose fear.

One whom wants to survive, excel, feel some kind of pleasure and adventure from this journey we call life should want to be able to consciously command things. To realize how much more one has to gain by believing in themselves- by believing in the possibility of incredible things happening, and by never allowing the confusion of life to create a darkness, or to not see the darkness created as beautiful in its own right. There will be so many moments in life when this positivism is forgotten, emotions and fear take over, but though we all must wander into this state of consciousness at times it is not a place any of us benefit from loitering around. The fear only exists when we allow it to exist. The battle of the mind can be tough but we would be wise to do all we can to not give up our freedom and enter knowingly into ignorant enslavement.

Those things which lay before me on the table, the objects in my pocket, and the objects in my hands seem abstract from the nature of life on this planet. The materials were gathered, designed and crafted into what they are. It seems as though objects of nature precede the ideas we form about them, yet that in respect to man-made objects the idea precedes the existence of the object. Man-made objects do not naturally occur but are the result of the course of prehumen-human evolution.

Now back to the objects surrounding me. The availabilities of possibility offered to all who came before me combined with my previous conscious decisions of my location, where I sat, that I even chose to possess such items and to carry them with me on this given day. I can begin to approach perceptualization of the randomness that occurs before human organization of that randomness.

If I close my eyes the reality of immediate perception says that everything disappears. Yet external to immediate perception the memory of the objects still exist within the caverns of my mind, and despite my lack of visual sense perception the world that was before me at the instant before I closed my eyes still exists. Object permanency tells us that even though we do not currently perceive an object in existence it exists independently of our immediate sensory cognition of it. Just as all those whom existed before us existed even though at the moment we cannot point to all of the details of their existence we know that there was existence prior to our own cognition of existence.

I think now of my grandmother, all of the emotions I tie to my memories of her are very real; and although she no longer exists in a living sense. Her presence at times can be as real as these things which rest before me. When the time of my own death arrives, my memories as well will disappear, as if none of it ever happened. Yet, my life will have occurred. I think that one's death is an end to their reality but not the actuality that their reality had stemmed from.

Part Eight

PHILOSOPHY

Who is Philosophy?

I have ventured thus far in this work openly exploring a number of philosophic ideas. The themes I more consciously intended to survey have manly been those concerned with phenomenology, existentialism and philosophy of mind. I have attempted to have experiment with phenomenology and psychological self-analysis and reflection upon the wide spectrum of my own human experience. Yet no matter how much I read, experience, or write I think that still no one knows who philosophy actually is. She hides behind the curtains, and always manages to just evade our thumbs cursory attempts at pin pointing her figure. She exists only in the shadows of our minds, curiously evading the grasps of our consciousness. She is therefore a mystery to most, and non-existent to some.

She is the embodiment of our search for knowledge, the progress that we make and our inability to comprehend anything in its entirety. She is the illusion of knowing, and the pursuit of ideas aimed at organizing that which is- into something both communicable and trans-mutative. She is the beautiful maiden whom we always wish to know, but never can gather ourselves close enough to ascertain. The pursuit then of the philosopher is the journey of inquisition into this goddess, and the impossible yet constant pursuit of her love and wisdom. If you pursue her only with logic, her spontaneity evades your configurations. If you pursue her with poetics and literary emphasis you over exemplify her, and exploit her in stripping the actuality down to mere fanaticisms' of what she may be if it were that you actually knew.

Can there be a bridging between these two camps of the heart felt spontaneous and the logically systematic? The logically systematic is primarily set upon organizing and controlling things and stuff using off a memory-based rationality. While the heart felt spontaneous prefers painting on blank canvas what it wishes for the canvas to contain. Differently worded the question could read can philosophy as both a science and an art coexist? The weather is rough, and one side is not clearly visible from the other. Yet each flies its banner and the settlers of its camp are heart bound to believing their institutionalization of philosophies' wise insights. Perhaps we should turn away from philosophy for a moment.

No. Never! She is a mystic goddess in all civilizations which recognize her presence. I present to you now a dramatization of the degree to which she is admired currently by man. She is often implied and rarely directly approached.

We dance around her with fanciful ideas, rejecting her as the center of our dance. We attempt to create a dogmatic world blanketing over the vastness of humanity, as if attempting to capture philosophy in a dress which we find pleasing so that she may be photographed and sold to market some new product. We make the screens she is viewed on rather than philosophy itself the center of cultural dominance in western society. Because we all view it on the same different devices we create an illusion of sameness and unity, while still feeling synthetically unique. When in each mind, house, street, block, city, state, and region philosophy is different. She has different eyes, a different smile, and she offers a different illusion. She is whatever we project her to be. To determine her to a static definition is to attempt to limit her into only perceiving the possibility of what some want her to be, rather than allowing her to be as she is; for she is powerful, raw, natural, and beautiful and for the power which resides in all these valuable attributes man wishes to control her and to objectify her for her wisdom.

The librarian whom guards the philosophers tools has accidently here become the editor, he whom allows or disallows access to content created by men who died long ago. He works in the movie studios, and television sets, at the publishing house, the newspapers, and even seeps his way into the internet. He attempts to control which aspects of the grand spectrum of philosophy are allowed to be considered by the public, painting her face the way he sees fit through layers of makeup and hours sitting on a computer editing via Photoshop. But alas although he may control the general societal perspective of this fair maiden, he cannot overwhelm her nature, she continuously reappears in ever-changing forms, and eludes even the keenest eye of the fascist librarian. She is right to do so, and man though thinking he is free, is merely a slave both to philosophy herself and also what the librarian allows him to view. He is more-over also slave to himself as he is possessed by his pursuit of her. He craves and obsesses in his search, hoping to capture it all, to synthesize the answers to life's greatest questions, and the moment he begins to think himself near to her complete comprehension, she shifts and moves again changing form, adhering to her eternal nature as a goddess.

No Escape

If we have no escape from our curiosity then we should learn to enjoy our propensity towards questioning. We seem to be not only a curious species but as well we have become quite an imaginative species. As far as we have been able to gather from life and our limited possibility of communication we can state that humans are the only species which truly has creativity. Animals make homes; such as birds which build nests, but how often does a bird act with cognitive intentionality to decorate their dwelling with flowers or objects of aesthetic beauty simply for the enjoyment of it being beautiful. This human fascination towards questioning and creative feats of imagination is uniquely human. Humans should be excited for the new horizons that their mind may find- exuberant about the new ideas and questions which may arise only from their unique perspective.

Never before and never again will the opportunities of this precise present moment ever exist! Each moments' very own fleeting nature makes it precious and valuable. Entering a pre-futuristic conception the possibilities should be explored with the upmost of our unique curiosity, fueled by our imagination as our minds reach out and grapple with existence. Even if we will never have the concrete and static answers that our misguided perceptions which both religion and science wish to assert for us, we still have an ever new playground with which our minds can stretch and implore creativity in its' reasoning. This playing with what is in front of us rather than the scraps which have been left behind by others is critical to pre-future conceptions, the preparation for the changes in the world that will come to exist in the future. To clarify these notions of momentary time perception the brink of now is the pre-future, and that which has passed is the past.

I think that we must however develop two particular virtuous traits in order for this enthusiasm towards curiosity and creativity to become truly pragmatic for the individual. There are two particular virtues for Humanity which I would like to discuss. The first virtue comes to me from French philosopher Michele Foucault, and it is *courage*. The second virtue comes from Fredrick Nietzsche, and is the *will to power*.

Courage is a word one might like to confidently exclaim they can explain and assert that they 'know' it's meaning. However, sometimes when we think we are acting outwardly courageous we are in fact failing to hit the mark of this virtue. Courage begins within, once we are honest with ourselves, we can have the courage to support those ideas in public forum or in action. The courage to be curious in a dogmatic world is not commonly found, for stemming from static dogmatists is a risk to our own survival both physically and socially should we assert the wealth of our truthfulness. The courage to be truthful in a world in which it appears the liars make it out with the cake and the silverware can seem unrealistic to ascertain. Each person should want to instill the truth within themselves, and when they have the courage to adhere to their own truths and not to buckle and fold at others assertions of truth which are just as likely to be deceptions as actual truths then we have the possibility of making the most of our curiosity.

In order to find this kind of courage to assert our curiosity, to proudly implore our creativity upon the world we must have something which lays even deeper in our conscious enacted. We must have our will enacted, we must want not only to be truthful, to be curious, to be creative, but we must as well will the changes and will the uncertainty that is associated with consciously existing in an ever changing world. I have enough difficulty understanding what this means in my own life and I could not begin to explain the actual effects that understanding what your own wills in your own life as my readers could possibly encompass, but I do know that I feel a good energy when I engage in truthful courageous willing. I hope with the greatest hope that this kind of self-trust is the cornerstone to evolutionary progress inside of human consciousness and society. These steps take great courage, and great will to be brought about. Cultivating these virtues can be complicated, but it is as complicated as you make it, perhaps being truthful and courageous in the assertion of wills upon the world is the most any one individual can do in their efforts to have a positive effect on the overall status of being-hood that one experiences during their brief existences, yet perhaps it can be so much more than that if we really will it to be.

3 Août

Saying goodbye to something which you like and feel comfortable with is never easy; I cannot help but think that the best things in life are the best for this very reason, they do not last forever. They must come and eventually they must go as well. However, the memories from these experiences last for as long as you choose to hold onto them.

Every day is new and all adventures grand! Should you choose to make them so by your own internal referencing. Life is such a wonderful journey through a world of possibilities. What path to take and what risks to put at stake? I think the choice is infinitely our own to make. Please for the sake of humanity live, and I promise to do the same.

A La Plage Avant la Fête

One person's mind as a singularity is in it of itself very complex. A given group of people and their minds are even more so complicated, and not always does each person when in a group context act entirely as themselves. Often times they act out their role, or the role expected of them, or the role they expect to be expected of them within the group context.

There is a war in my own mind, trying to calculate these subtle differences of humanity within the confines of my conscious stream of reality. After a series of odd encounters and occurrences, I sometimes think my great aspirations, such as the potentiality for human consciousness, is just that, and aspiration and not reflective of actuality. Yet when something good happens, especially simple acts of kindness and goodness I am reminded that humanity does exist, and that we are all active agents of humanity. The shared sense of humanity as a reflection of love and good wishes towards fellow humans still flourishes even amidst the controversy of group societal existence. Though there is an ever-existing capacity for the greatness of humanity, it is clearly not always actualized. Often times our fears overwhelm our courage, our confusion overpowers our wills and we fall into a state of being that is in actuality less than our full potentiality. We may yet find refuge in the sentiment that in time all things will pass.

"Are they (humans) really complicated? Or do they just make things complicated? Life is supposed to be easy, but we make it complicated" – Mathew Kalahike

We constantly muddy up the clarity of our own humanities as we weave deep and deeper webs of thought about the way things are and even more-so about the way we project things ought to be. We overthink and under-think situations and we overact and underact according to the mean of virtue (in the Aristotelian sense). We are prone to fallacies, discrepancies, and accidental wrong action. It is not that we intend to be wrong, but as a coincidence of attempting to be right we are inevitably often quite wrong. This is embedded in our very natures as human beings whom are active conscious agents in the world of things.

Perhaps life too is an accident, and the duty is left for us to decide what to do about occurring in the midst of our own accidental existences. We will accidentally make the right choices, and accidentally make the wrong choices. Our perceptions provide us with the illusion of determinacy. We can make up the ideas of wrong and in doing so we de simplify making choices and taking actions. It is our reflective associations which apply the factor of value, it is our own consciousness which judges and decides upon what is right and what is wrong, while in the world of things external to our conscious evaluations things just are. We say that something is wrong when it has an effect that is not desired, an effect that provides us with no or less benefits than another, and we deem things as right when we are at least satisfied with the results of something which our minds intercepted and we or someone else has chosen a course of action which offers some apparent reward.

"We are born into chaos, and a world without meaning but human beings have the ability to create meaning in the world which we were born into." –Mathew Kalahiki

4 Août

What more could one need to be content than connectedness itself? If a means can also be the ends it is in itself complete, and has the power to proliferate itself. What an awesome power that would be!

5 Août

Trouble with trains, and warm weather, my bike tire exploded with a loud bang. Some people may be confused enough to think that their reality of life is happening in everyone's immediate realities. You cannot plan life nor can you control it. Life just happens and it is up to us to be content and make of it what we can. A life cannot be out of order, but one can have trouble dealing with the psycho-emotional effects of feeling alive, thus causing the cognitive-emotional disorder. This is because life is weird.

I question whether or not one can be content without being happy. Mathew thinks contentment is momentary while happiness extends into longevity. Myself I think of it on the contrary, that happiness is momentary and that contentment prevails over time. We do not know anything.

6 Août

All of the colors and vibrancy of life are not necessary for beauty. Even in the darkest of places in the blackest of black there is immense beauty to be found. We must take the time, have the courage, and the will in order to find this beauty. There can be music in the silent moments, health in sickness, and joy in sadness. The stressful moments come, and eventually they pass. When these moments pass, and you remain open to life, something wonderful arrives and takes the place of the darkness, and you can then bathe in the light. Even if only for a short while, until the darkness returns.

Ce Soir

What an amazing day I had. My morning at the hostel in Annecy that I checked into last night was interesting. In the afternoon I talked with a cool traveler named Rob, he is an American from Carolina living in Los Angeles primarily, but right now he is in France on his way to Iceland. Traveling and staying at hostels is so interesting, you meet so many different kinds of people on all kinds of journeys and paths in life all with the courage and the will to step out of their elements and explore. This quiet medieval town is a great place to relax, enjoy the beauty of nature, and yet have the intellectual stimulation that is so inherent to the French culture.

It was raining lightly when Sarah picked me up. We drove around the lake to a nice quite place outside of town. We had a few glasses of wine and I had my last swim in Lac Annecy with her. We took a drive to the base of Mt. Semnoz for a quick hike where were played with billions of ants. I am not kidding the ants were everywhere! The raw power of nature of this area is overwhelming. The mountain towers above all, and it is draped with a forest which is ever renewing its own vitality. Small creatures scattered among it are the stewards which keep the forest alive. These ants all have a job and an importance in the ecosystem, in the flow of life, even if in their own existence they are not consciously aware of it, they are preforming a great service, and they make enjoyment of the forest possible for so many other creatures, and humans alike.

We then left the countryside and went back into town for dinner at a restaurant her friend operates. Dinner was followed by drinks at my favorite place in all of Annecy, La Buvette du Marche for a digestif, café, and champagne. It was fun although sitting on the terrace, puffing away at cigarettes I could not help but think how much I would miss that place, the people who work here, the people who frequent the café, and the overall ambiance and atmosphere of that area of la Vielle-ville Annecy. I had what seemed like only moments to soak it all in, and reflect upon my appreciation of my experiences there and how much this trip had allowed me to grow, and learn about life and all of humanity in general.

We then took off in her car and drove to her apartment. She drove in the rain blasting French music, laughing and dancing the entire time. I had to leave in the middle of the night to collect my belongings at the hostel. I walked back through the wet and empty streets of Annecy to the hostel. I freed my bike from the gate to which I had tied it up. The tire was blown and I was to depart from Annecy the next morning. My bike had served me well during my time in Annecy but I had no need for it where I was going so I wrote a note and left it tucked into the bottom of the bike seat. The note (originally written in French read):

"Hello! You have such good luck today in finding my bike! I was a student here for the past few weeks and this bike got me everywhere I needed to go. The tire blew up and since I have no more need for the bike I

do not wish to undergo the repairs. So this bike, since you have found it is now yours. All that I ask in return is that you do something kind/generous for another person."

The bike was locked up along a fence just outside of La Bibliothèque, across from a park and the lake. I was certain that in this location someone would find it shortly.

When you grow to love something, or someplace, it can be so hard to say goodbye. Your memories and your emotions rip at your cognitive faculties and cause a mix of emotions to come flowing upon you. The experience of life is not always easy but it can be incredible! Eventually we have to pack up and leave our beloved, safe, comfortable pasts behind and venture off into the future sun. You never know what great happiness's and adventures are waiting for you around the corner- When you finally muster the courage to selflessly give yourself up to life, and to live in the pre-future, you may just find out how much life has to give back to you. La vie est une fête, va danser!

Ideological Flourishing Vitality

The path ahead is always littered with uncertainty. We can imagine all kinds of futures, yet despite even the most accurate predictions, we are constantly surprised by the way things play out. The human race is particularly new to the fields of technology, from machines which made work lighter, transportation infinitely more possible, to electronics which enable people all over the planet to communicate in real time like never before. We have no idea what introducing technology to children is going to look like. My own generation is going to be the last to remember life before satellite TV, computers in every home, cell phones, social media, streaming viral videos, and ever visible sources of advertising. Our parents would not have thought the advances which have occurred in their life time to be possible, so we should expect to be surprised by the events and the inventions which appear during our life spans.

Unfortunately as we have made our advances over the past century we find that at threat are vital resources for life. Resources which are increasingly diminished by an overpopulated species addicted to technology, sources of energy, and energy processing. We do not exist independently to our environment; we are all parts of greater existence. The same stardust that makes up the planet makes up our own bodies. The flourishing of all forms of life is a necessity for the continuation of human life and thusly for the continuation of consciousness. If we wish to dive deep into our individual explorations of consciousness we should pay an allotment of attention towards that which makes life possible. Namely for example: bacteria, microorganisms, insects, plants, and animals, etc. etc. whom all work together in earth's ecosystems to sustain each other. The hyper-oppressive needs and wants of humanity must then be mitigated in our attempts to ensure the continuation of our own cognitive existences. We would benefit from finding new marks of virtue in humility and unselfishness in order to obtain that which we need to keep the vitality of life flowing.

We should have the courage to unlock life's mysteries in

ever new and changing perspectives, to eliminate our fears of the unknown by accepting our limitations of knowledge. It is a difficult task to open up the heart so that the mind may flourish. I think that the intellect wishes to preserve itself above all things, yet it is the love which stems from the heart which has the capacity to ensure future existence of life and consciousness. When we extend our humanity outside of our own selfish desires we stand to accidently receive benefits though the intentionally selfless helping of others on their journeys'. That which works, must be that which works overall not only that which works from one perspective; and that is my view of social-pragmatism. The forcing of <u>one perspective upon all others</u> is precisely what social pragmatism must fight against. The balance of self and others is hard to establish and even more arduous to maintain yet ideologically the possibility looms over the horizon.

In an idealistic world one would love their environment and all of the participants in it. The simplest premise is self-love. If one can love oneself, then they can love others. If love for loves sake is the focus of the individual it can pour forth unto others- creating a microclimate in which both the individual and the groups which they collectively compose can begin to make progress. It may take centuries even millennia for us to hammer out our differences- to void ourselves of the 'evil' and pains that are associated with our prejudices. In the spirit of honesty I feel compelled to admit that I am not always able to abide by this creed in my own life. Yet despite occasional failings I still do not hinder myself from dreaming of the consequences of this loving symbiotic pragmatic efficiency and what both life in the general sense and humankind have to benefit from its serious consideration and implication.

A complex understanding of evolution involves not only physical factors of mutation, change, and flourishing of genes through genetic populations, but as well, in regards to higher intellect species and more specifically towards humans it includes socio-emotional and cultural development. Social groups adapt to the currents of changing conditions, in doing so traditions and taboos are formed and members of the group are expected to adhere to these concepts of social normality as if there were absolute truths. Rather these practices for the greater part of the universe's existence had no grounding and no application. These concepts of normalized morality were non-existent in the early days of human evolution but arose within particular populations at particular points in time as necessary methods for group survival. That is to say that by following these guidelines the individuals within the group fare far better as individuals because they adhere to social contracts- and furthermore having stronger individuals benefits the entirety of the group; it is from this symbiotic attempt at social pragmatism that the first laws arrived.

Historically these laws were often labeled as the decrees of deities or from *god*-like political power holders, and thusly from the get go were intended to go unchallenged. However, circumstances arose for individuals in which their own survival or pleasure quests pushed them towards testing the strength of the staticity of these fundamentally evolved and non-static ideals. Ideals which are not only not so static as we were told they are but whose only possibility of coming into existence relies on a non-static nature of perception and social applications of consciousness. This may seem as though my message here is embedded in riddles but in fact what it is attempting to show is that there were periods of history which occurred pre-historically, periods in which these concepts did not exist. It is due to the nature of the existence of things (including ideas), which stemming from their own temporal non-existence allows them the right to their temporal existence.

We are barred from absolute knowledge, seemingly locked out of the gates of the great temple of wisdom. This leaves us to make the difficult decisions of when to violate traditional social normalities due to the overwhelming gains of their utilities for either the individual or the society at large from a change in course. Also thinkers are challenged with deciding upon which changes in the tradition normalities should be undergone, for what justifications, at what times, and for whom. These arise as grand questions to which there is no right or wrong answer. Neither one person nor one group can ultimately make these decisions for any one person, let alone a social group or all of mankind-though inevitably many will try. I think that thinkers will be driven time and time again to try to either preserve those traditions which existed since before their time- so long as they feel that they or their society will benefit from them, or make alternations as needed. In making these alterations they inevitably will at times feel compelled to make these attempts to change the status quo in order to fulfill their own needs and desires.

In an overview of the foundations of Western Philosophy in Greece one could argue that all pre-Socratic philosophers were speaking from their own relative vantage points in their empirical investigations, and for the most part there is a trend for the ethical evaluations to be formulated upon that which can provide justification for ones actions as a response to the social climate which restricts or contradicts the actions which they find individually pragmatic. As the discourse of western philosophy continues the story is much the same. Social climates of pragmatic relevancy shifted, and those whom full-heartedly applied their intellect to the assessment and continuous thought about the conditions and relations of things have found ways through their investigations to create a communicable justification for those acts which they feel advance the survivorship or pleasure drive fulfillment of most often themselves, and secondly what will, from their perspective, enhance the flourishing of the social group(s) of which they are a counterpart.

It seems as though all minds apply their ego-centric forms of rationalism upon their own uniquely acquired relative empirical information. This is exactly what the evolution of the human mind has conditioned itself to do. We gather information and we calculate by our own innate senses of logic and then we make decisions of action according to our adjustments of previous existing social modules for normality. Our memories of the past give us a reference point for our rational, and for our ethical evaluations of action, yet the pre-future activities of the mind occur every time we make a decision and then act upon it. We are always intending to find gains in our attempts at pragmatic expansion, yet only time and the results of our attempts can provide us with sufficient hindsight to judge whether or not some action was truly pragmatic in nature- and not merely being called pragmatic because we want to believe that it is.

I think that most persons conduct actions under the justification that they 'felt it was the right thing to do'. But what is rightness? Are these matters not so infinitely relative to the context of any given person? For example one could spend their whole life writing explanations in German of the complexities of their ideology of rightness. So when the finished work is brought to a non-German speaking woman in Indonesia and it is told to her that in this book exists the complete and entire definition and evaluation of rightness. She from her cultural and linguistic perspective attempts to analyze the material and internalize it for her own advancement, she finds that she cannot understand the symbols and she has gained nothing but a book which she cannot understand and thusly has nothing to gain from. This exaggeration displays the futility of trying to determine anything for others and to force it upon them just because we will it so earnestly to be true for ourselves, that we are willing to wager that it must be absolutely true for all other thinking minds.

For each of us perceivers yesterday, today, tomorrow are all days- conglomerations of time reference and time-specific distances, linked together by memories. If what I write here makes no sense for the past, it might make sense in the current moment. And if it makes sense in neither past nor current, it may still provide something for the future.

8 Août

With my bags packed, I checked out of my hostel, and after a few hours in town all my important goodbyes have been said. I now sit here at the café for the last time. I spent so much of my time sitting here, watching people walking the stone streets, conversing with my friends, reading and writing. I feel such a deep emotional connection to this particular part of town. Though I spent many hours at my school, the lake, and at my host families house, there is something about this part of town that was so amusing and lively, it is something I will always greatly appreciate. During times like this, one can be so torn between the past and the future- fearful even of living in the present moment. I need this time to reflect as I try not to shed tears. When I leave here I must be rid of my fears and freely venture off into the uncertain future.

I know that as much as I will miss where I am and where I have been there will always be new people, places and adventures waiting for me. I am trying to make it to Paris this afternoon so that I can make it to Amsterdam by tonight; I have to sneak onto my first train as I have no reservations.

I digress; leaving the town of Annecy my heart feels as though it is in chains. Ahead looms a fantastic city of freedom and liberation. I think that I am finally ready to take the step, the first step will be the most difficult but all which follow will grow easier and easier. Goodbye Annecy!

I wish I could crawl into a cave of ignorance and hide from my overflowing emotions, but for me this is not an option, I choose and freely chose to accept and deal with the reality of change- the inescapable passing of moments and differentiation of experience.

Gare du Nord, Paris

What an experience I had getting to Paris and now at least I am on my way to Amsterdam. I snuck onto a TVG train with my rail pass but no reservation in Annecy for Paris. After a few stops they finally decided to check tickets. I told them I had no reservation but had tried to get one with no luck. I was fined 5 euro. I thought this was pretty reasonable given the situation and I gladly paid. No one sat near me and I slept a lot on that train, tired and emotionally drained from leaving my mountain home in Annecy.

Eventually at Gare du Nord I was able to get a reservation for a train from Paris to Brussels, one from there to Rotterdam, and should arrive finally at Amsterdam Central fifteen minutes before midnight. I was eating at the train station when I met a nice Australian couple. Claudia is an artist and has a 'garage' studio in a small town in the south of France. Not only does she enjoy sharing her creativity with the world through her paintings but she shared with me during our conversation that on this trip she is also sharing her experiences more intimately this time by traveling with her husband. Apparently she usually travels to her studio alone, and works there for some time before returning to her husband in Australia. I thought it was really adorable how excited she was to share this with me before her husband sat down and joined us with their lunch.

People can think and feel so much in life on their own yet it is all the more rewarding when you find the method, time, and right person to share it with. Her husband and I were discussing that fact that people are people, and we all feel the same things and encounter similar problems, despite country of origin. He continued to explain the importance of art and the aesthetic experience of a means of breaking barriers and sharing humanity. It really put art, aesthetics, and the human condition into perspective for me. I was also so appreciative in this moment of the artist, of the one whom so courageously reaches out to share the intimacy of their existence through whatever medium. To me I have always felt that artists make up a very special portion of the overall human population.

I stepped out onto the streets of Paris for a last quick smoke before boarding. A young man approached me and asked me if I had a cigarette, I in fact had plenty of tobacco in my pouch and I rolled one for him. He told me I had an accent as we were speaking in French. I told him of course I have an accent because I am an American. He was surprised. After telling him where I am from and where I am going he told me that I have a nice life, I agreed. I may not have always seen it that way from my perspective, but I appreciated how I felt that he genuinely meant it. He shocked me as well when he stated that I am an interesting man. I thought that he is interesting too, even if he does not think so, he just hasn't realized it yet. I told him I live for the experience and that he should as well. His name is Boris and it felt really good to have a simple but real human connection once more; even in a city as seemingly at times void of humanity as Paris is. I had to cut the talk short to get on my train, which I did… just in time.

Perseverance

Weak moments are inevitable; we will find ourselves sad and feeling worn down. An important part of the reflective process is to allow ourselves the time and space to heal. Once we have readjusted and figured everything out, we are ready to come back again fighting the good fight. There will be moments where we will feel overwhelmingly limited and even defeated by our environment or our circumstances, and at times possibly even by ourselves. Yet it is how we shake off these problems that consciousness encounters, problems stemming from and existing within our own consciousness, that show the true strength of perseverance. This works on both a personal level within our own consciousness but as well within the sphere of relationships. There will be times when we argue and disagree with people we love, but when we wake up the next day and we chose to remember not the pains of yesterday but the hope and future of tomorrow and embrace those important persons with love that our real conscious strengths are utilized- and the love continues to grow.

There is always someone worse off than us, yet the test of humanity is in how we attempt to overcome adversity and face our fears. If we do so with positivity and a progression towards the greater pragmatic good we should fare better than if we allow ourselves to be conquered by our fear evoking memories. As we have explored we do not always control our circumstances but we do have some control in how we view and react to them. We can step deep inside of our own consciousness and make these choices. When we are beaten down by the world but continue keeping on keeping on we find resilience. Some will struggle their entire life, yet wake up every day willing to do what they must to survive, those people deserve respect and not to be pitied for their difficult circumstances, for even if we are better off than they, we have much to learn from their struggle. It is those who give in to wanting whom should be pitied, those who do not want to be strong but to make others be strong for them who truly deserve our pity more than they are deserving of our help. Every day is a new day, and should be embraced with all the love and possibilities that exist- fully embracing its newness.

La Prix du Liberté

11 Août

Amsterdam is such a marvelous city! I was so lucky to have my friend Bobby to guide me around the city; it was a lot different this time around than my first visit was. I once more got caught up having too much fun touring the city, it seems as though the entire time I forgot to write. After all I had spent countless hours during conversations with Bobby pulling back and jotting down note after note in my journals, I felt as though I didn't want to do this when there was so much for him to show me, and only a few days to see it all. I arrived back in Paris questioning again, what is liberty? I find that freedom is far from free.

At the base of one of the world's greatest architectural feats, the Eiffel Tower, an exhibition of liberty, that I find the same thing which I found everywhere else- namely a price. Even entrance to the tower relies on admittance fees; lines turned to crowds almost mobs of tourists and lovers as they rush towards the booths to buy tickets to the top. After the tickets are purchased the tourists and lovers merge again into the lines to ride machines all the way up; all in the name of liberty. Crawling all over the lawn are economic slaves to the ideology of liberty and freedom. They believed without skepticism the arguments which propaganda told them. That it would be worth the journey north from Africa. You cannot buy liberty, especially not in a cheap icon peddled by immigrants desperately struggling to survive in a foreign land that they now call their home.

Tired and worn down they hungrily search for the paper marks of imaginative liberty, or at least the money which society likes to think will somehow lead them to liberty. As the tides shift and the channels of prospective 'liberty' notes return to their hotels, the hunger grows. On the surface, it appears they are hungry for money, but in reality they are first hungry for food and a place to sleep. And only secondly for liberty, and lastly they are hungry like all of us, hungry for the world- that it may one day also be theirs. It is so sad to watch as I begin to realize that the first thirst is far enough from their grasp, the second and third will likely for them as for most always be a dream dwelling far off in the future.

For those who find the money or 'liberty' that they search for, they sometimes get so lost and enslaved in their search that they never get to actually enjoy the freedom it provides. When you choose for yourself and reject society's wealth standards and expectations and live in contentment as a currency for liberty rather than money a currency for power, you will find a new form of wealth. I think that one may possibly find liberty, if it is that liberty has some substance which can be found. I question now if it is better to search for something that you do not know exists or to continuously search for something which you know exists but that you can never have?

12 Août

I am still trapped in over-congested Paris, but feeling like I have better luck today. Perhaps what I really needed last night was some sleep after a long day traversing the city. Last night I met a girl at the hostel named Chelsea from Huntington Beach, which is very near my hometown. She was pretty, friendly and talkative but I felt she lacked real human depth. Everything with her was on the surface. I could feel that she was worried about her appearances and what I might think of her. Her fear kept her from being free. I returned to my room after speaking with her for a few minutes, eager to finally get some rest.

Today is the final day of my voyage in Paris; I want to go to the Louvre to see artists who found outlets of expression despite their fears. Maybe I can learn something from them. I did not pay a visit to the Louvre my first stay in Paris, and I felt it would be a shame to have stayed in the city and not made time to experience it. I am excited because today, much like every other day is a new chance for life and experience, I want to be open, to learn and to live freely. I think that being free then must take a lot of courage. Courage to me is not the same as to not have fears but to act in the right way despite those fears. So I leave this Parisian café with hopes of a real experience; something deep, something liberating. Curiosity...

There were a few other persons at the Louvre who actually took interest in the art, and not just in saying that they had been there. Many more however go to run through a museum so they can say, "yes, we went there and saw 'that'", with little to no attempts at deeper understanding of artistic modes of expression. I did at least get a chance to view human evolution through a distinctly European lens by viewing artistic expressions across vast spans of time and from many different regional consciousness's. In my opinion the most particularly marvelous sections Greek Sculpture and pottery. The ancient Greeks had such a refined and deliberate culture at such an early age of human evolution, in every respect I feel as though they were truly ahead of their time.

As time passed technique and refinement of designs increased, yet the focus stayed relatively the same throughout. Human discomfiture with life and with existence, followed by an immense need to produce distinguishable works of art which attempt to display the battles that exist within the mind, the spirit, and within society as a collection of minds and spirits. Usually a perfect serene woman is depicted, with faces of strength and compassion, or powerful male figures squashing demons and monsters. Modern art can be more bizarre and have more difficult themes to distinguish, yet the perceptions of normality have also shifted from what they were as we came into this modern era to encompass a variety, grandeur, and simplicity that art had never before experienced. Perhaps as well the abstractification processes displayed in many forms of modern art is necessary for understanding how art has developed in brotherhood with new mediums, techniques and messages.

Back to Los Angeles

August 13

What a grand adventure! I saw so much, met so many persons, and learned so much more than I ever thought I would from my travels. It really must be better that these things, experiences, come and the moments pass. Our favorite memories and happiest moments are worth more because they do not last forever. Their futility adds the value of their momentary existences. Imagine if the earth stopped spinning and all things on it as well as time froze for eternity, what a pitiful way it would be to spend existence frozen in one moment. It is by our good fortune that movement exists, and that at times it brings about life, and death brings about even more newness and change.

It can be hard to recognize how great a feeling, an exchange, or a moment is while it is still occurring. If however it is possible to be momentarily conscious, that is to be not concerned with the past, or anxious of the future, but existing in the moment open to the thoughts and feelings evoked from the uniqueness of the moment itself- then this way of experiencing being seems to have a propensity towards freedom from psychologically based fears, is closest to liberation, and is conductive of the experience of happiness which when amassed over a lifespan can form an ideologic but possible road to human contentment.

I think it is because of the futility of the passing moment that memories are still some of my most prized possessions. Though many of these memories and their associated emotions will not necessarily bring me any closer to happiness nor content, they hold lessons, history, ideas, and most importantly they are the closest thing I have to all of the people I ever loved, to anyone I felt close to, shared a friendship with, or sometimes just a few glasses of wine during a last night in a big lonely city. This is where my humanity lays, and tomorrow I will chose where to place my consciousness next. I remember before I left on this trip, all of the students I was to travel and study with from Hawaii were asked to answer what one thing they would want to have while traveling abroad. Everyone else replied with an object, however, I, myself replied that I never wanted to be without my sense of humor. I think I carried it well with me throughout my travels, and that it kept me open to many of the experiences I had while traveling. I realized that always and forever, I am living in the now, and that even if my sub-consciousness shields my consciousness from the reality of this, it is still the actuality of my being that I am here, that I am present even if my mind may begin to wonder as it so frequently does.

Thinking of Thoughts

Something we all have, something we all see differently, something which may exist externally to humanity, something we carry with us throughout our lives- consciousness. I have so far managed to elude an actual definition for consciousness throughout this entire work. I have mentioned facets of consciousness, and its relation to the real world yet putting a finger down on consciousness is difficult. This is due to the vastness of consciousness and conscious experience. I could only do so much as describe it from my point of view as the limitations are great. Consciousness is so independently inclusive that even to describe it I am limited by it, I cannot see what rests outside of it- the things it conceals so well. Perhaps the best way to describe it is merely to encourage you to think about what it means to you. So go ahead and do that, don't stop, keep going, for the rest of your life.

Return to the Aina

August 24

Home is wherever you want it to be. A safe place in the world, family, a friend, or a space you made inside your own mind. It is where you know the seas and the sky, the mountains and the roads. It is a place to think, to love, to laugh, home is a place of safety and a place of reflection. Aloha Aina.

I was sitting on the beach in Hawaii once more. I sat there reflecting in the warmth, the humidity, the softness of the sand and the comfort of each crashing wave when I experienced my bliss, my home, my love, my existence. Feeling feelings ever so indescribable, yet deeply memorable. We should want these happy moments for ourselves, we can make every day wonderful. Even with this power, the problem of other minds still exists, and we must become wise enough to accept that we can never make someone who is decidedly unhappy happy.

Life is Weird,
Life is Wonderful,
Life is Good!

Once one fills their self they begin to overflow
and they can shower themselves upon others.
Our lives' spent as a forest of mountains, living in the clouds.

ABOUT THE AUTHOR

Daniel Martin is an academically trained philosopher from Orange County, California with a degree in Philosophy from the University of Hawaii at Manoa. He is a lover of all things nature. His favorite philosophic themes are Existentialism, Phenomenology, Pragmatism, Evolutionary Psychology, Ancient Greek Philosophy, Chinese Philosophy, lastly but far from least Practical Philosophy. While studying as an undergrad it became apparent that while reading surviving texts of some of the greatest thinkers in human history that the entire possible knowledge one could gain from these texts would be utterly wasted if never put into application. That is when practical philosophy became important.

During Daniel's undergraduate studies. He was the president and facilitator of the philosophy club at the University of Hawaii at Manoa called P4E (*Philosophy for Everyone*). The group brought about practical applications of knowledge to solve a number of philosophically inspired issues from a multi-dynamic and plural perspective. Skepticism is essential to practical philosophy, one must thoroughly evaluate information and make sure that it checks out and is actually applicable in real world situations in order to make practical use of their philosophic wisdom. This non-static approach to epistemology (the study of knowing), is explored in depth through the philosophic considerations expressed in Life is Weird.

The big questions for practical philosophy arose: How can we live our lives enjoying ourselves and our existences, loving every moment? How can we formulate a *Philosophy of Awesomeness*? That is, how can we create our own systems of thought that understand our unique relative perspectives, our longing for happiness, and mitigate our needs and desires such that we fulfill a reasonable amount of them and create a positive out-pact on greater existence? It takes a lifetime! We seem to be in luck, a lifetime is exactly what each one of us has. Both the book *Life is Weird* and Daniel's blog on *Things Stuff and Consciousness* approach these questions of existence, of mind, and of flourishing awesomeness.

Printed in the United States
By Bookmasters